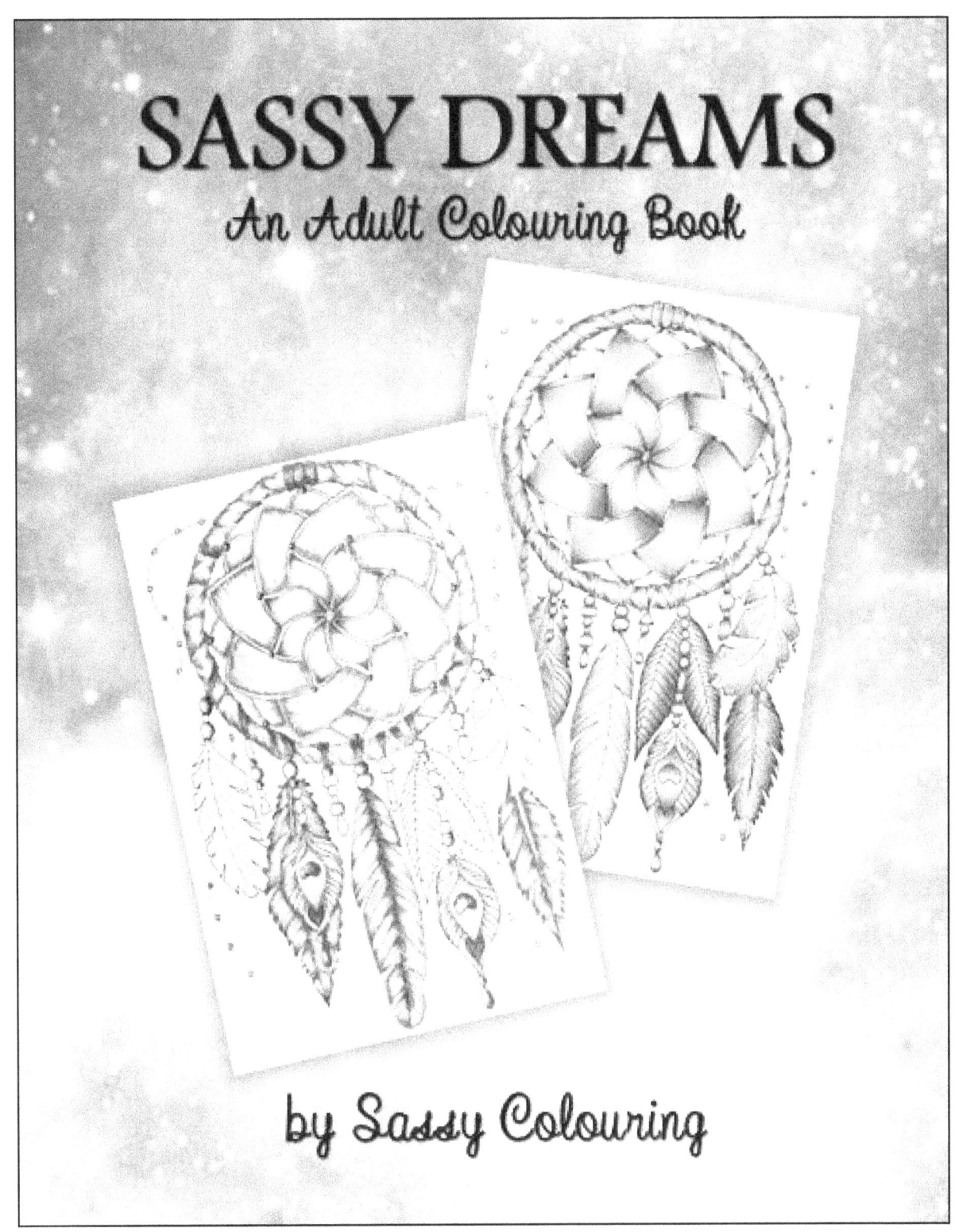

SASSY DREAMS
An Adult Colouring Book

by Sassy Colouring

The cover for Sassy Dreams was coloured by two wonderful members of the Sassy colouring team. The left was coloured by Donna Pecoraro of New York and the right by Nicola Tagger of the UK.
Thank you ladies for such beautiful images!

A massive thank you to my wonderful colouring team – I would be lost without you!
Donna Pecoraro
Nicola Tagger
Tina Dahldren
Jill Haworth
Colleen Diamond
Beth Cook
Louise McKie
Michelle A Turner
Veronica Baartman
Suzzanne Axten
Honor-Marie Watchman
Michelle Kelly
Naomi Clair Brookes
Sonya Griffin
Tracy Catron

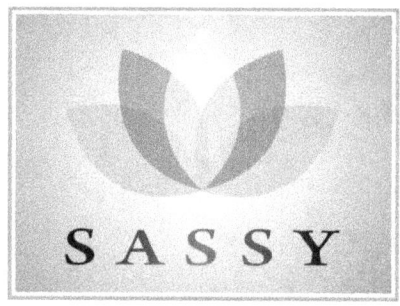

HAND DRAWN BY

SASKJA COOK

What better way to relax than to colour.
Whether you're looking for a way to unwind or a new hobby, colour therapy has been proven to be an effective stress management technique.

I love to draw and I love to see my pieces brought to life by each colourists unique take on them. Each piece is a collaboration between us, my drawing and your colouring.

Please feel free to share any finished pieces on:

www.facebook.com/sassycolouring

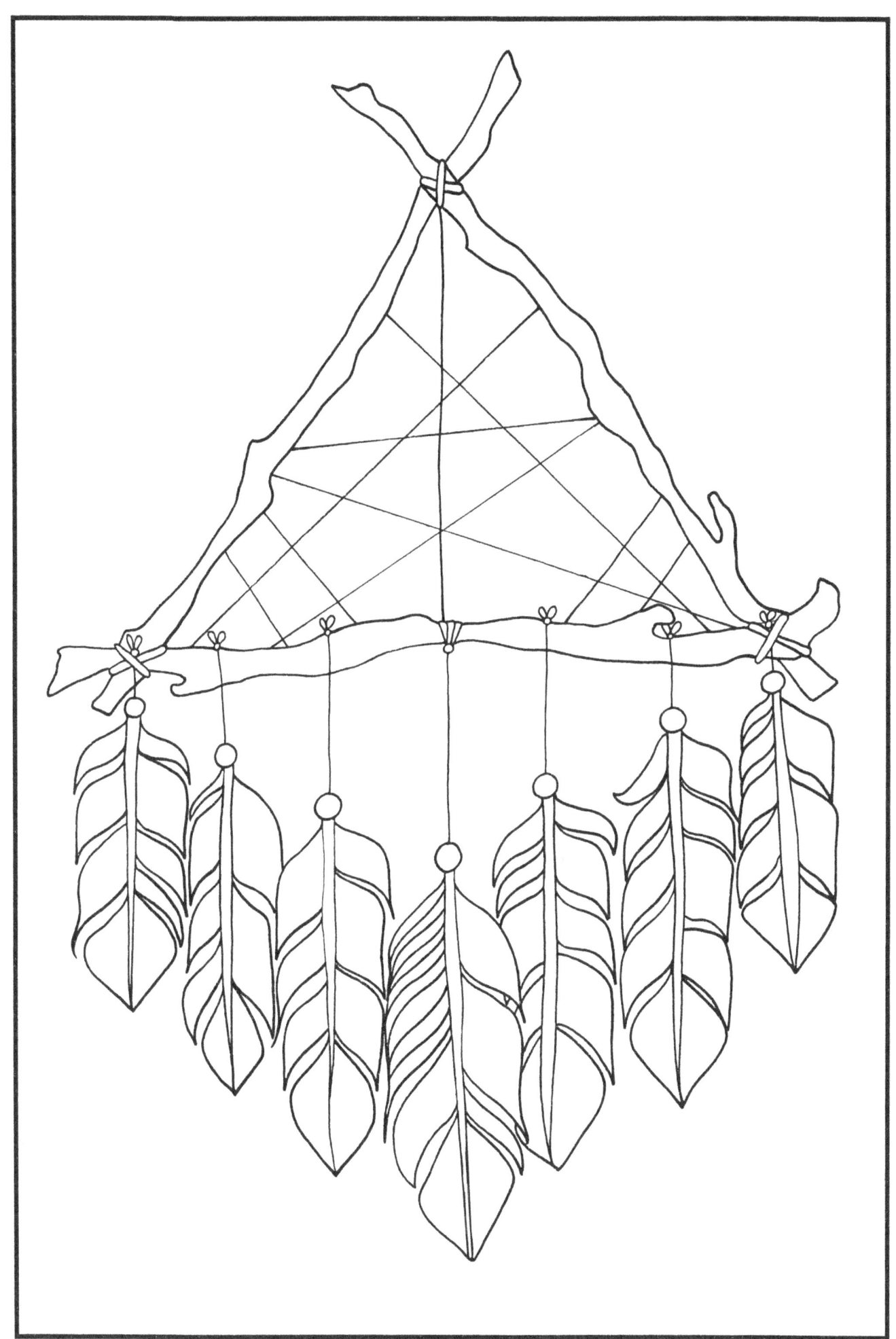

Always Dream!

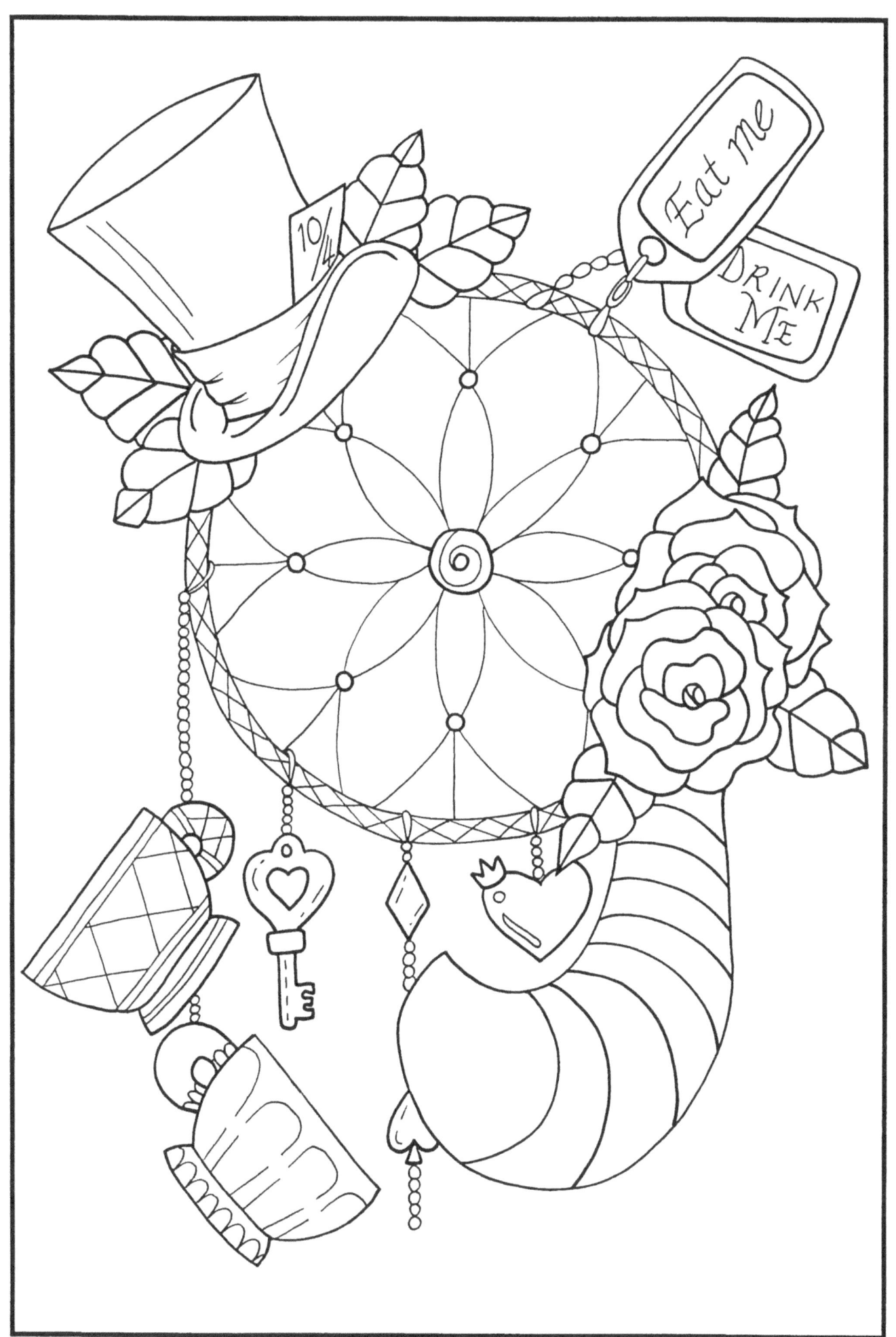

Wonderland Dreams

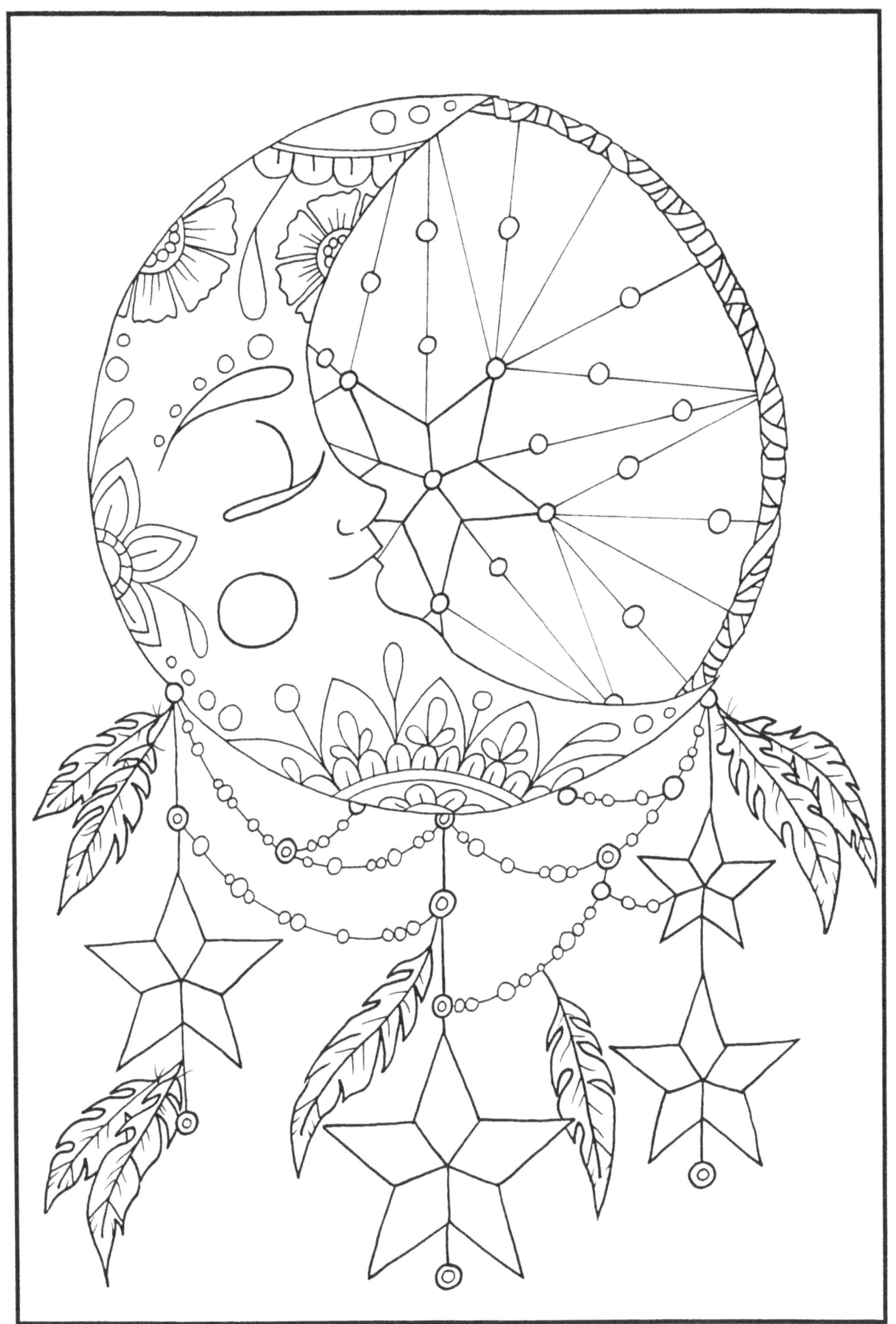

Dream to the moon and back

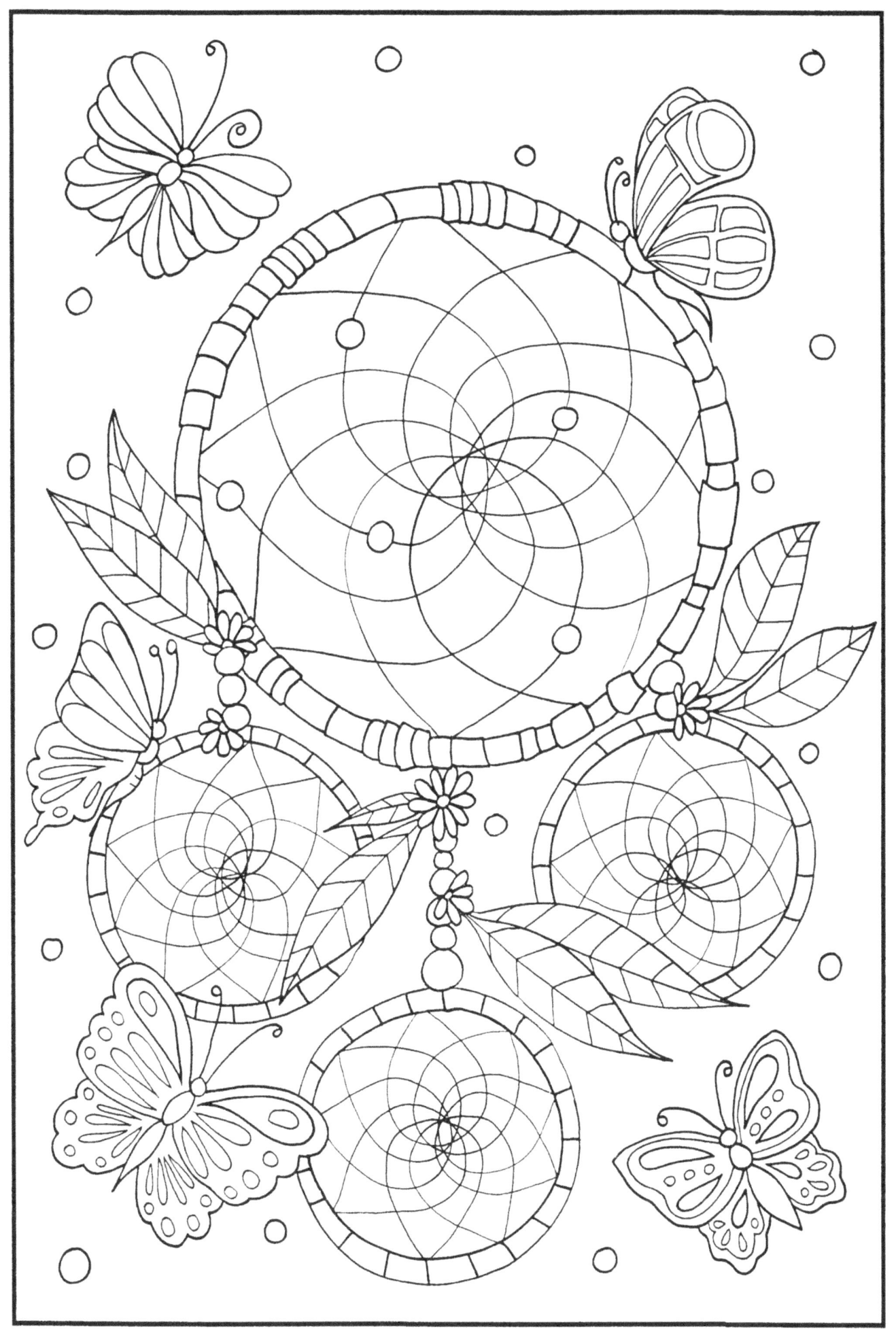

Butterfly Dreams

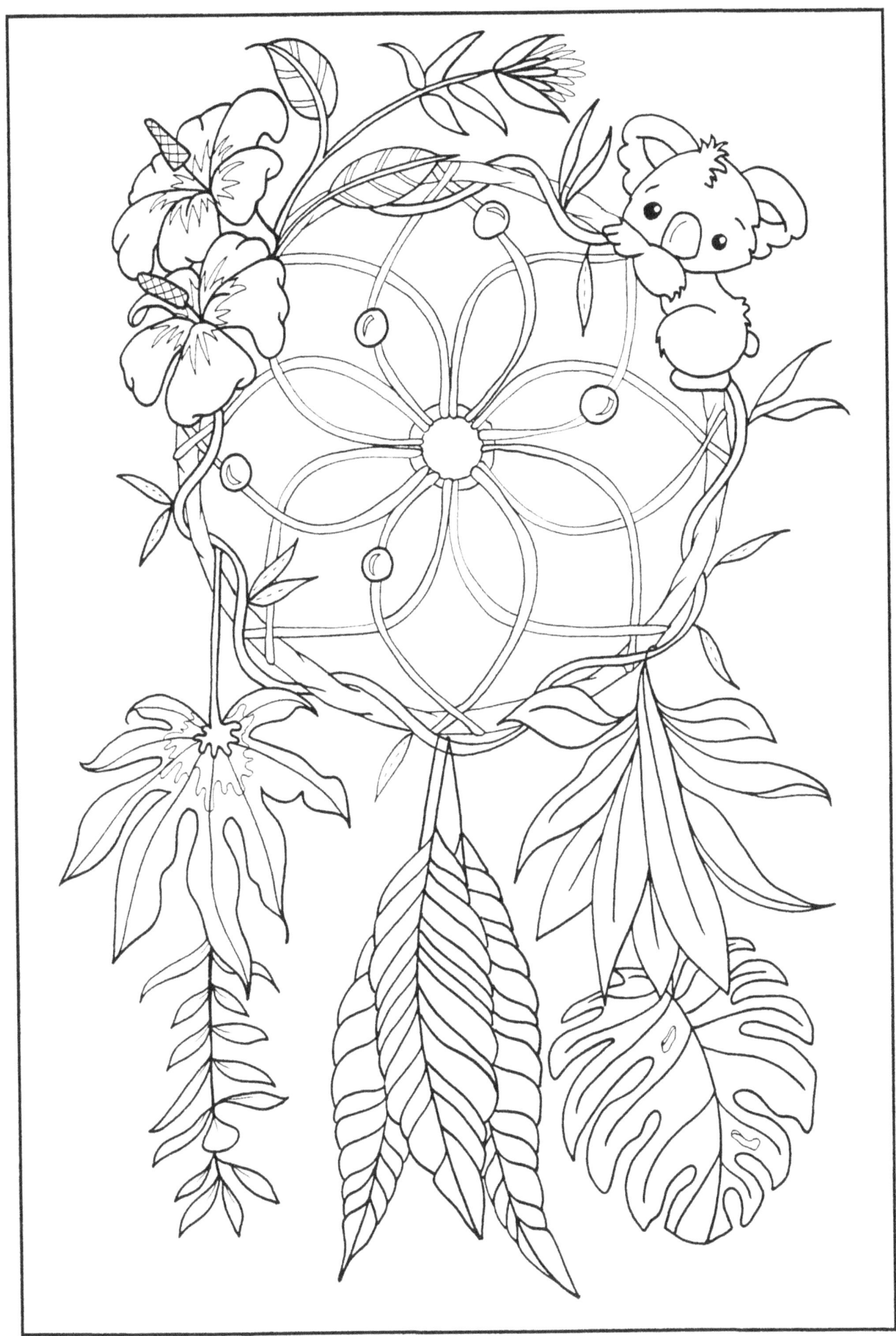

Tropical Dreams

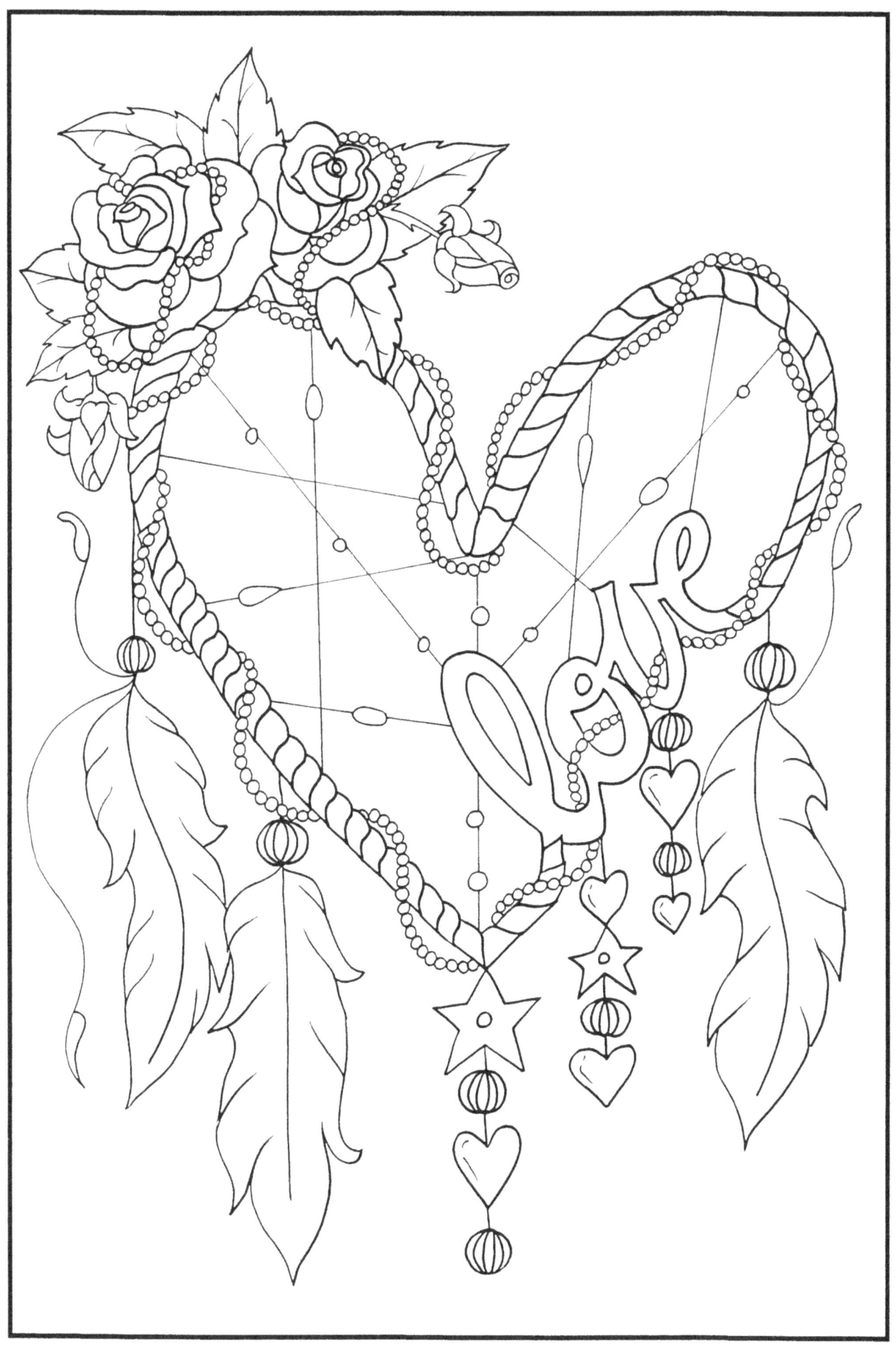

Find the love of dreams

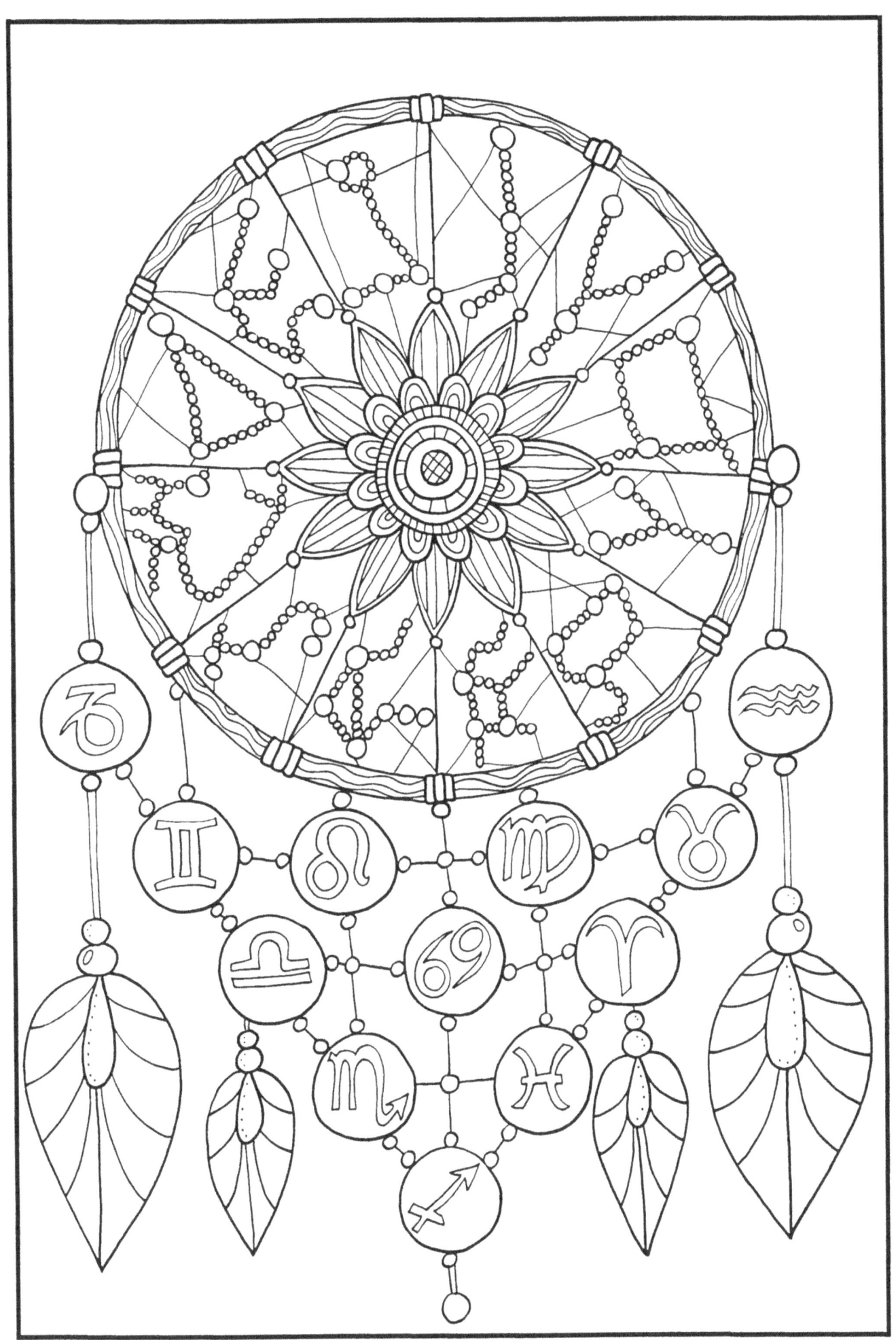

Zodiac

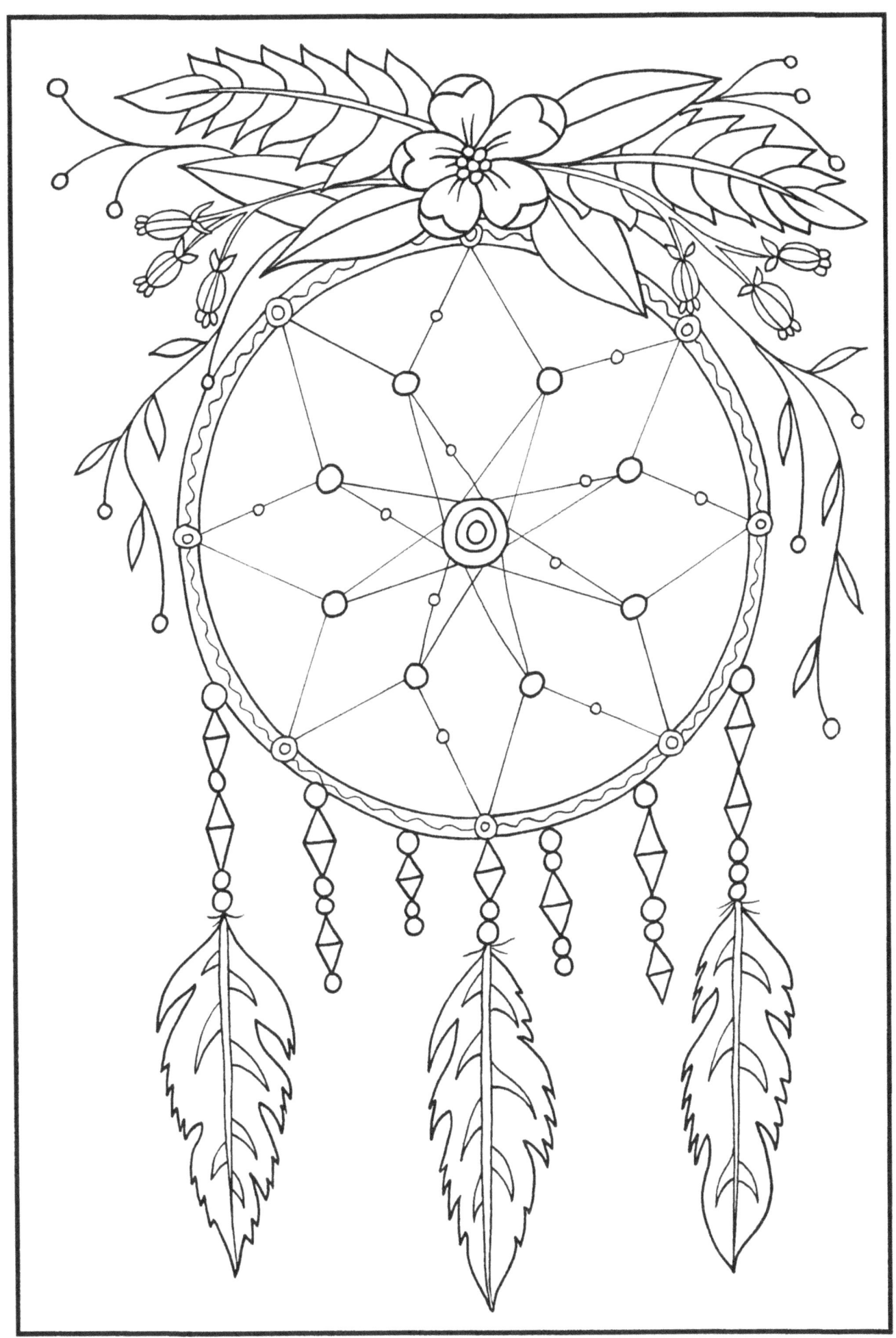

Flowers and Feathers

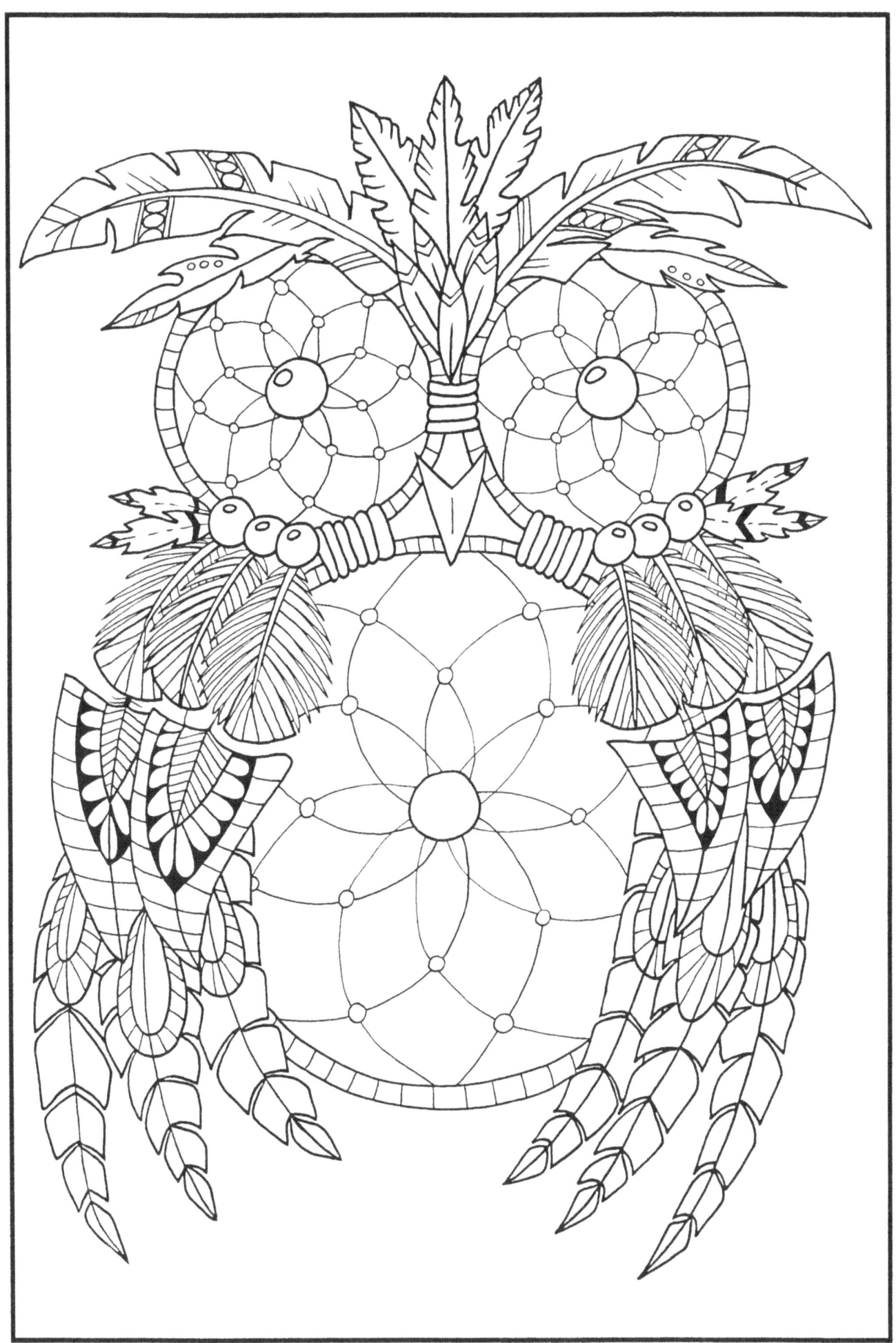

Wise Dreams

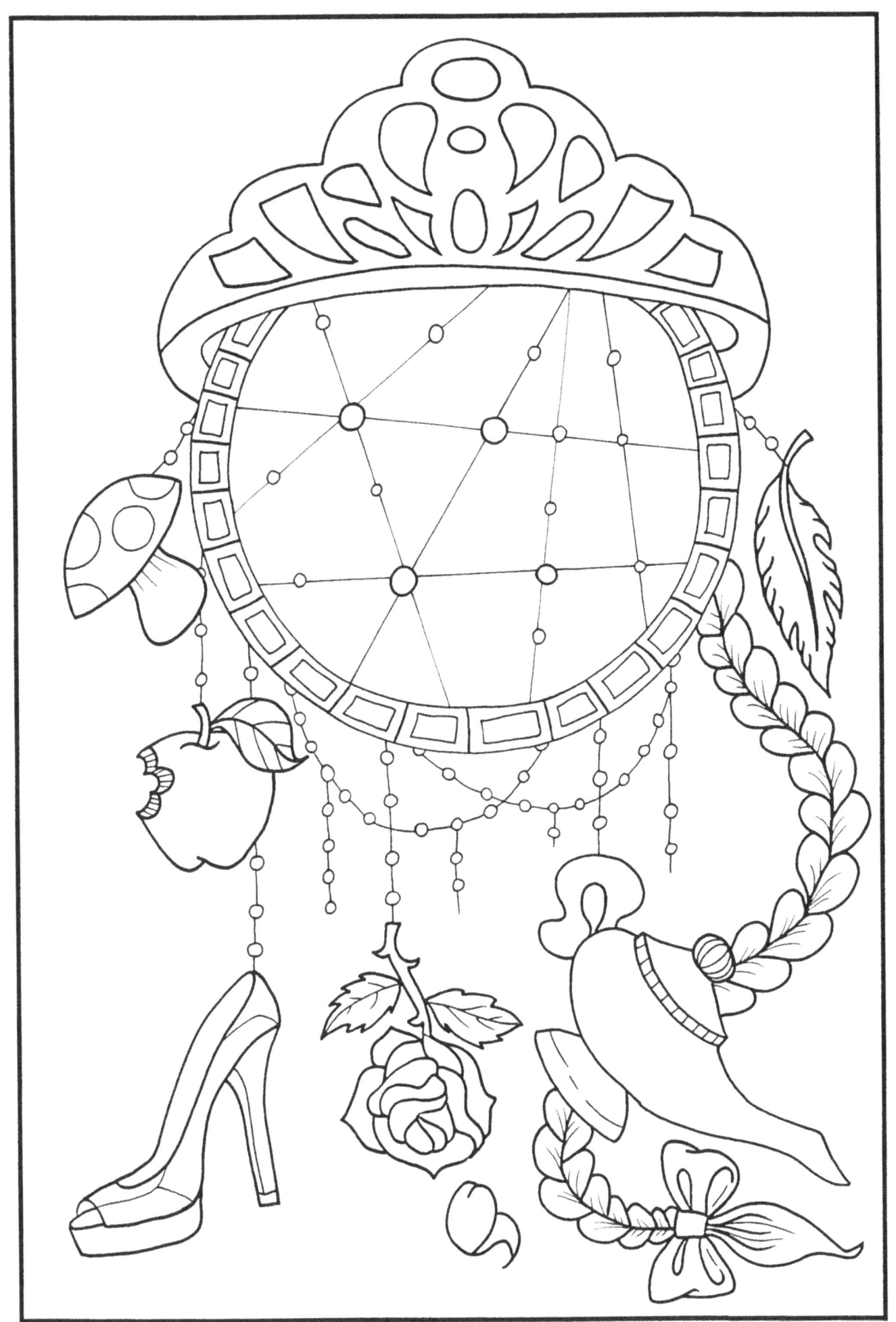

Enchanted Dreams

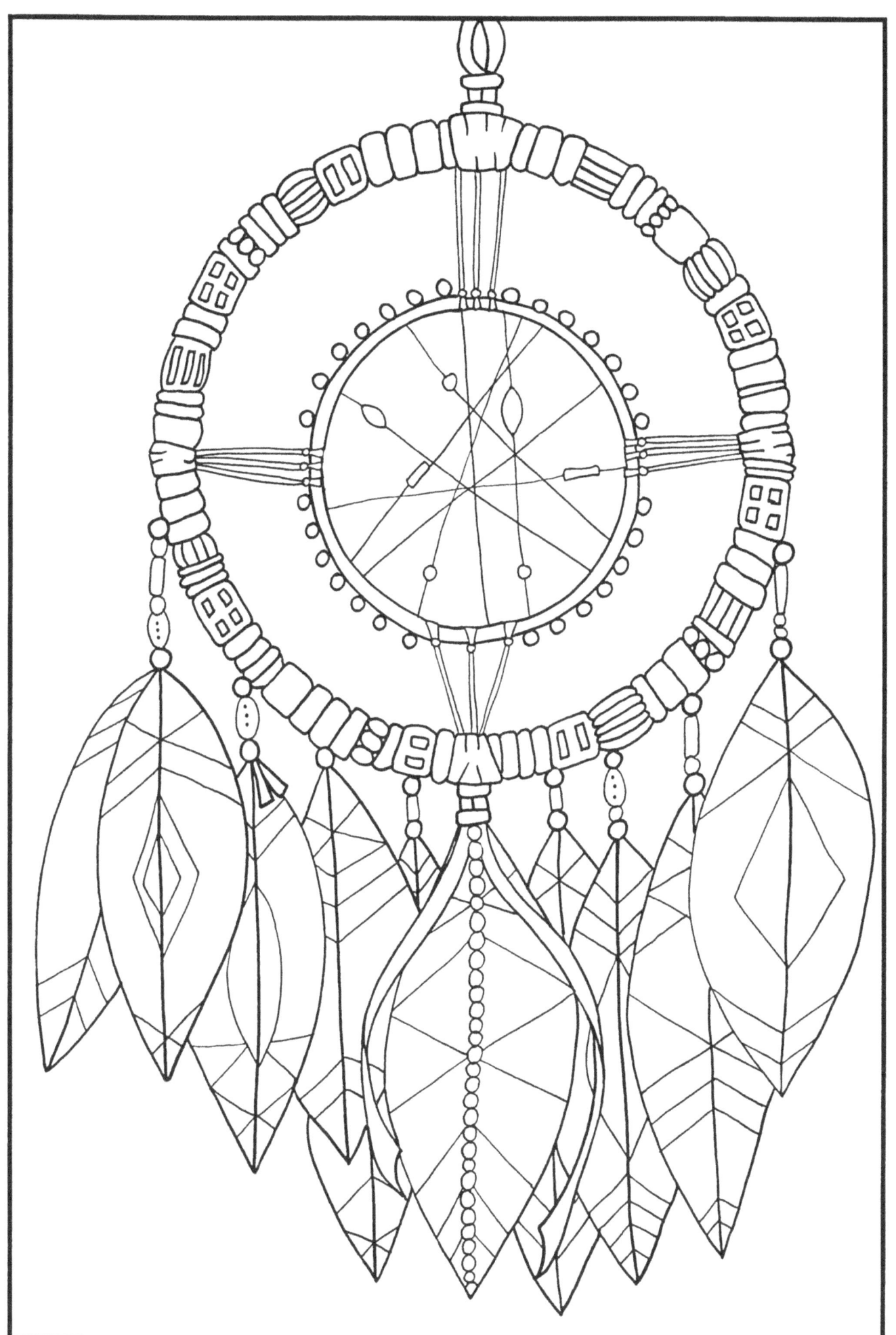

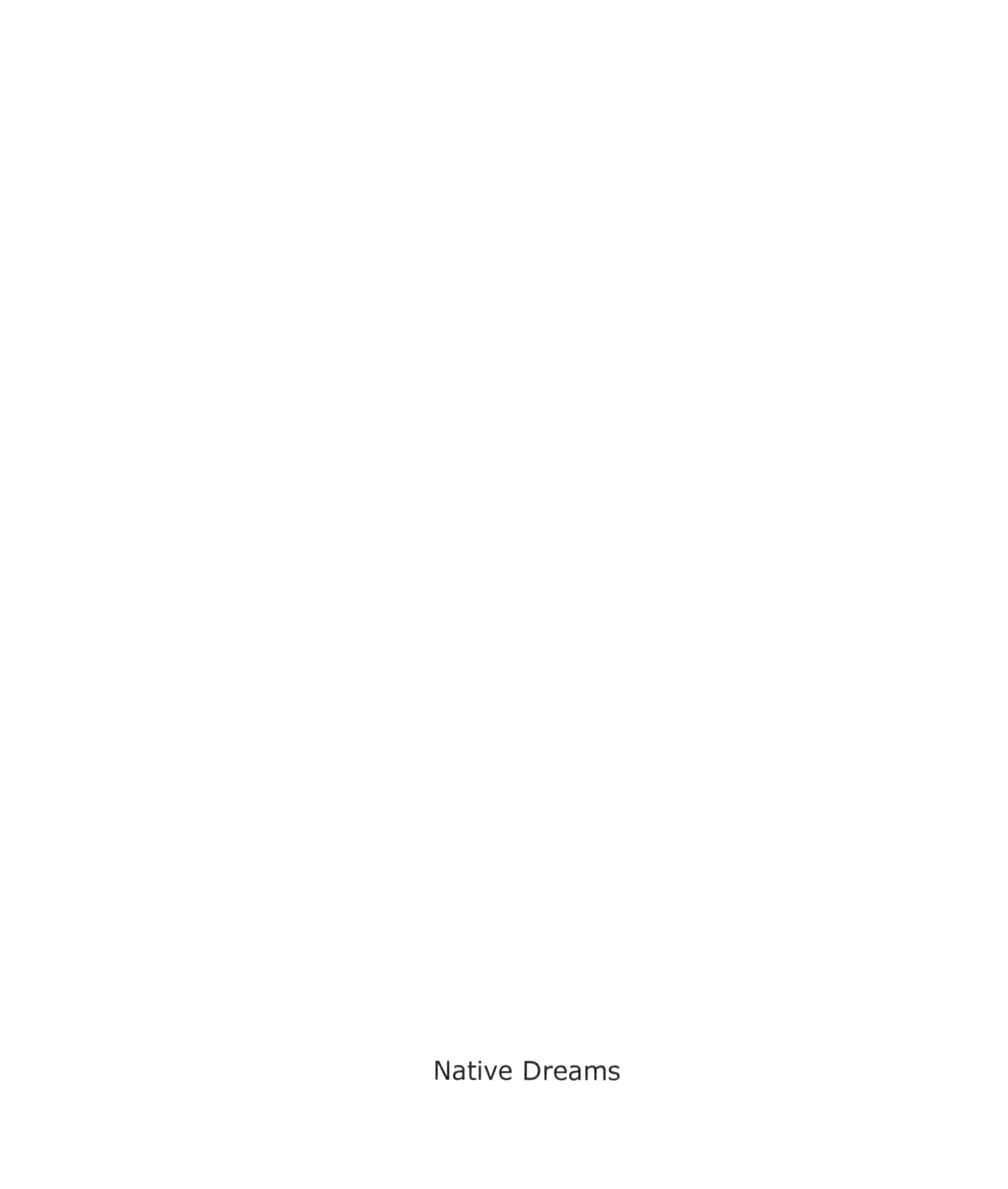

Native Dreams

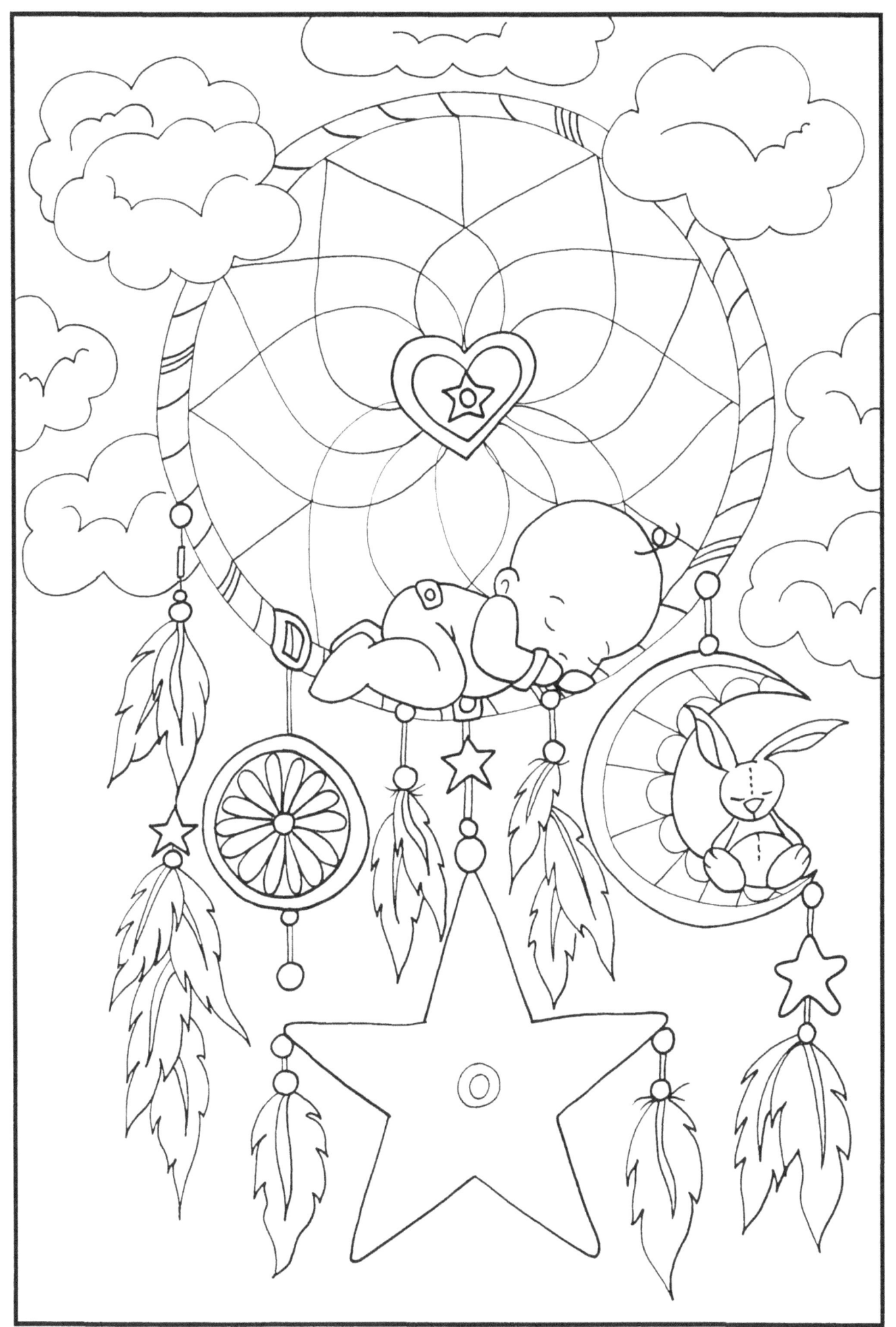

Sweet Dreams

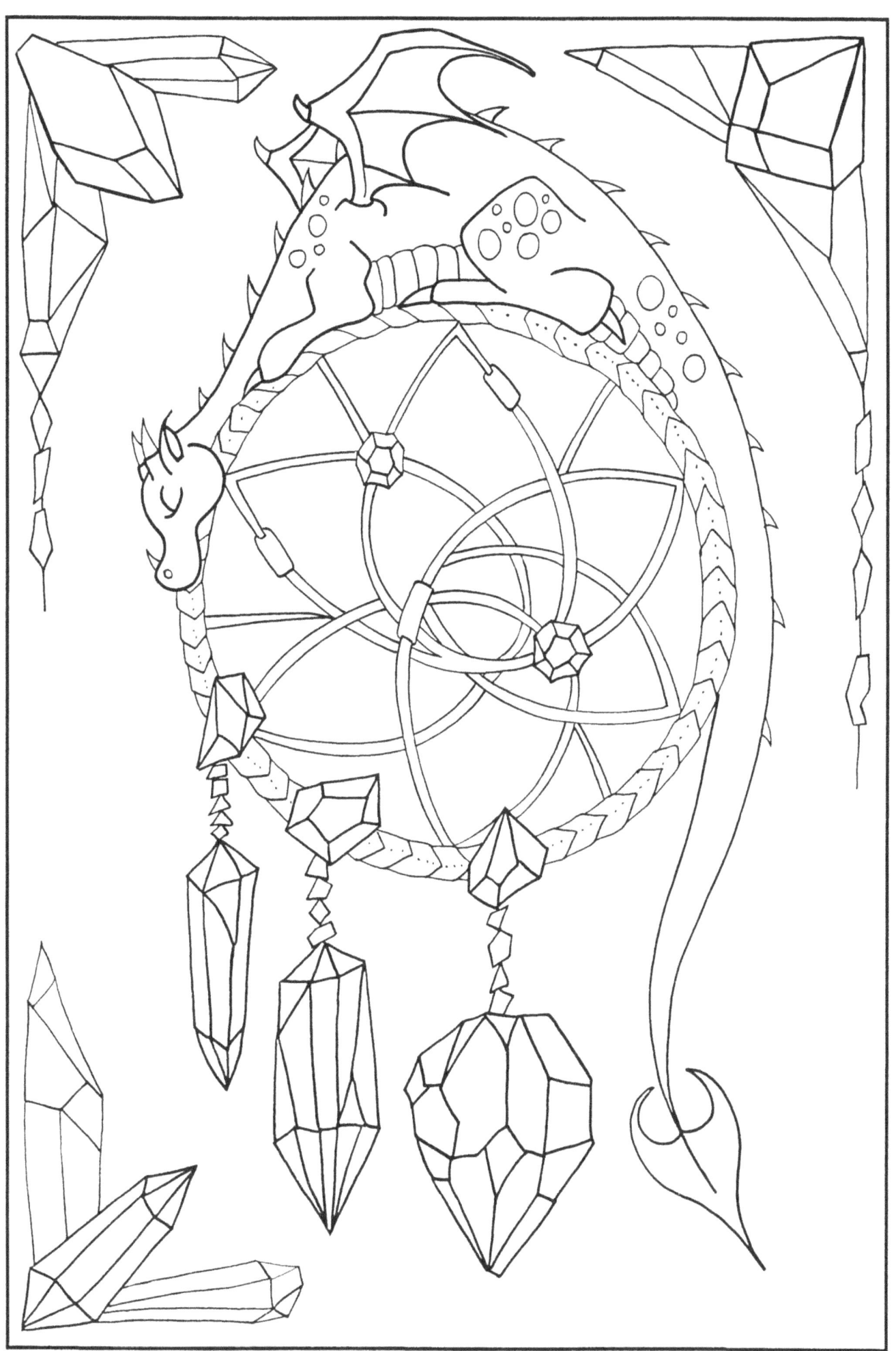

The Dragon

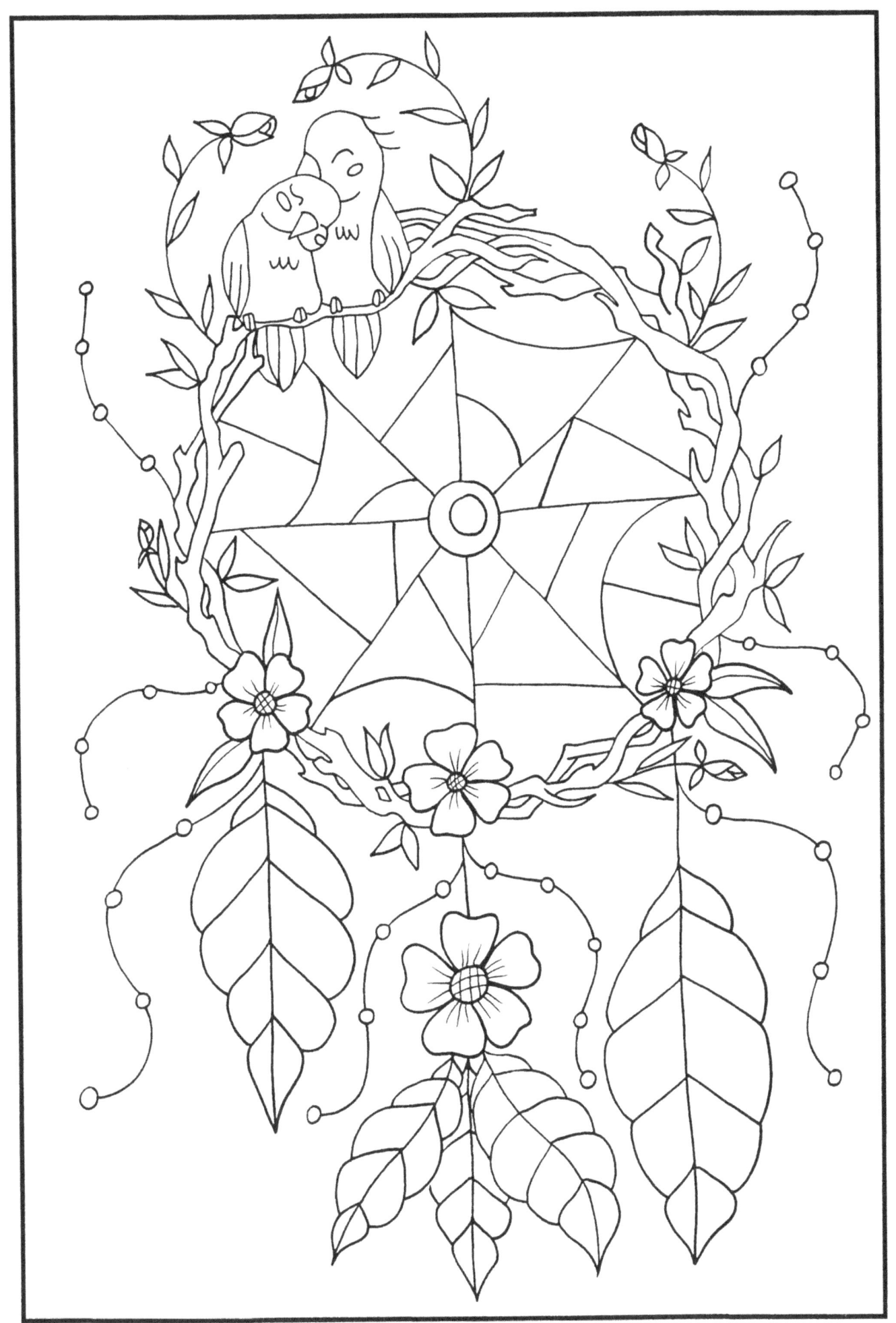

The Love Birds

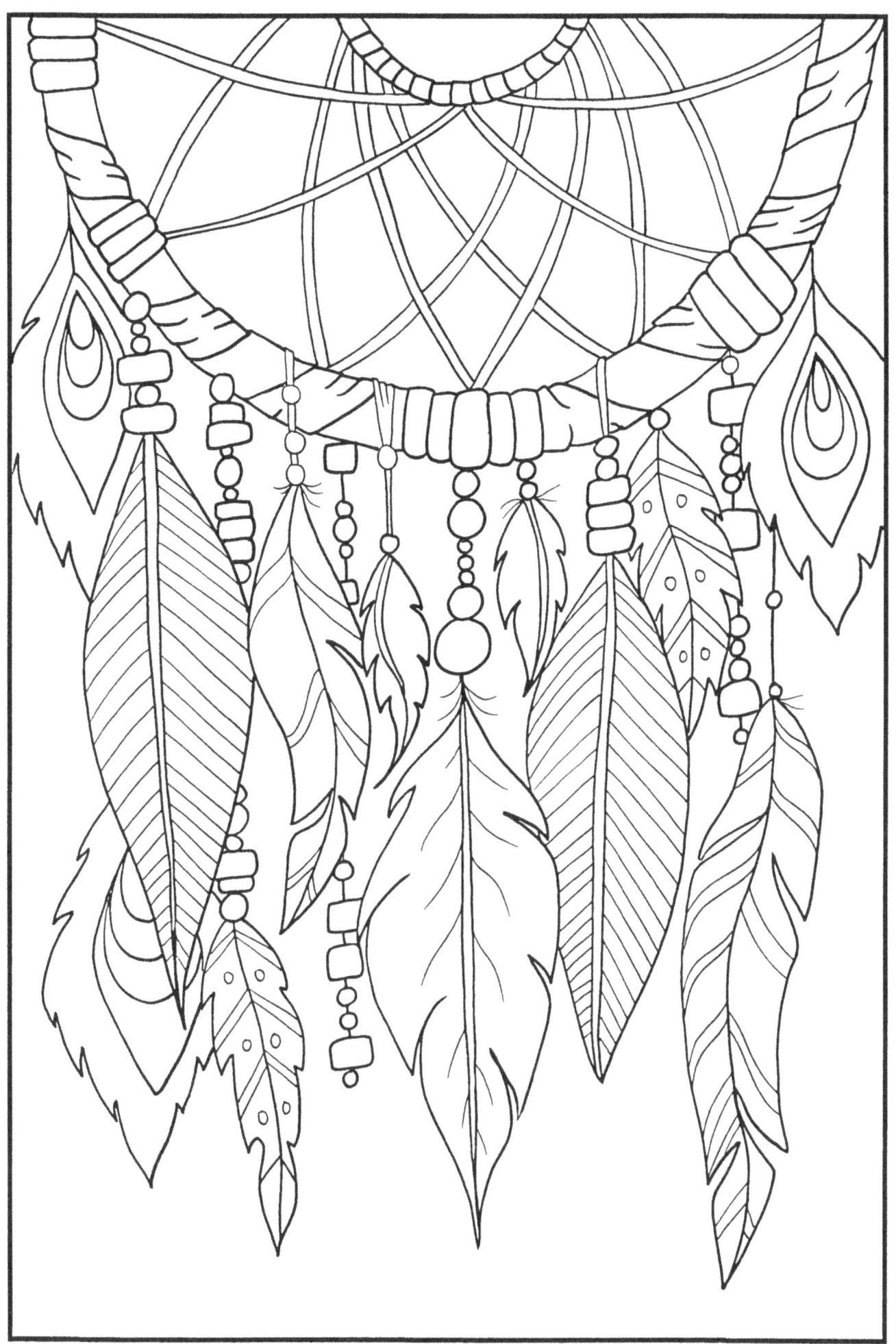

Flurry of Feathers

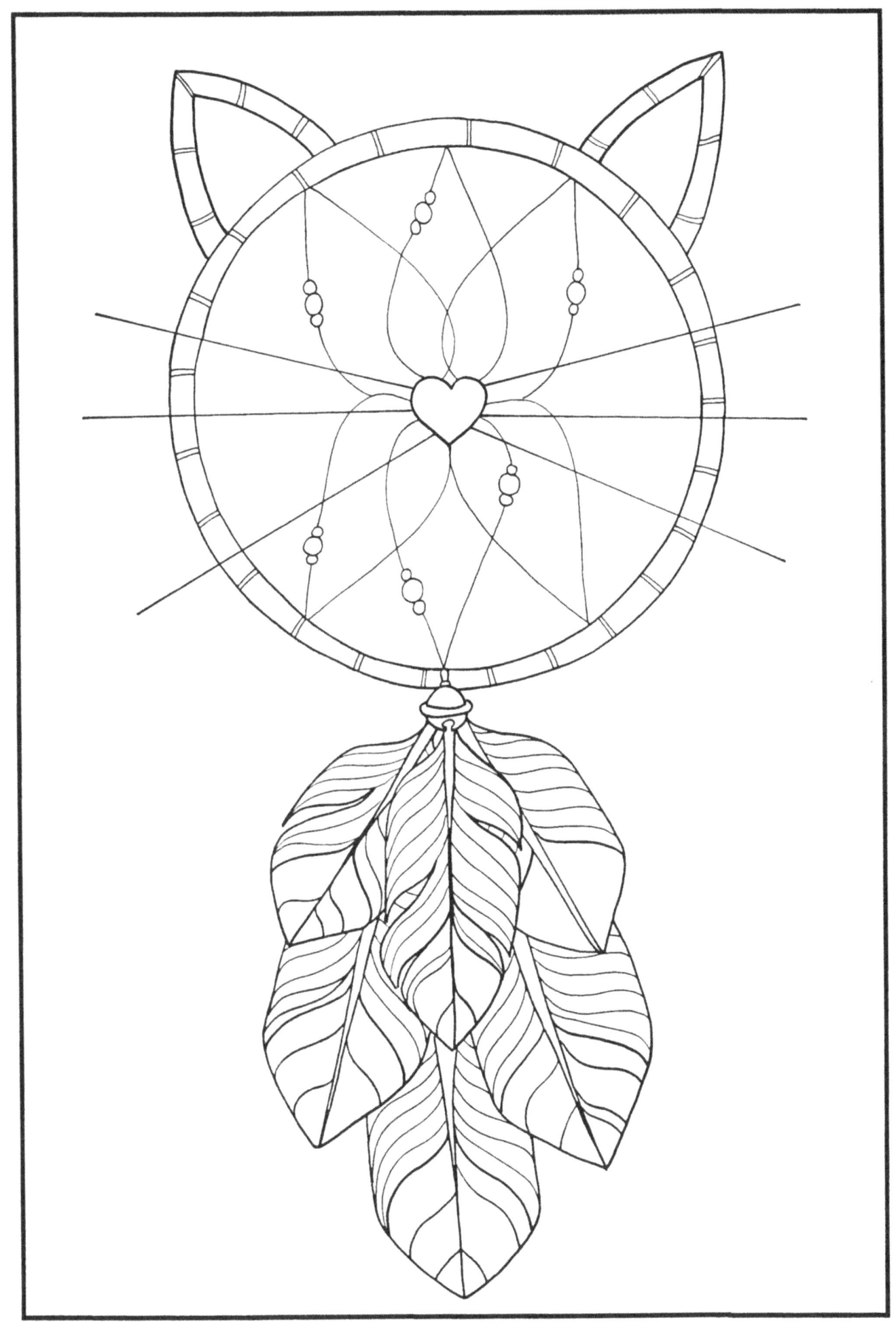

Cats

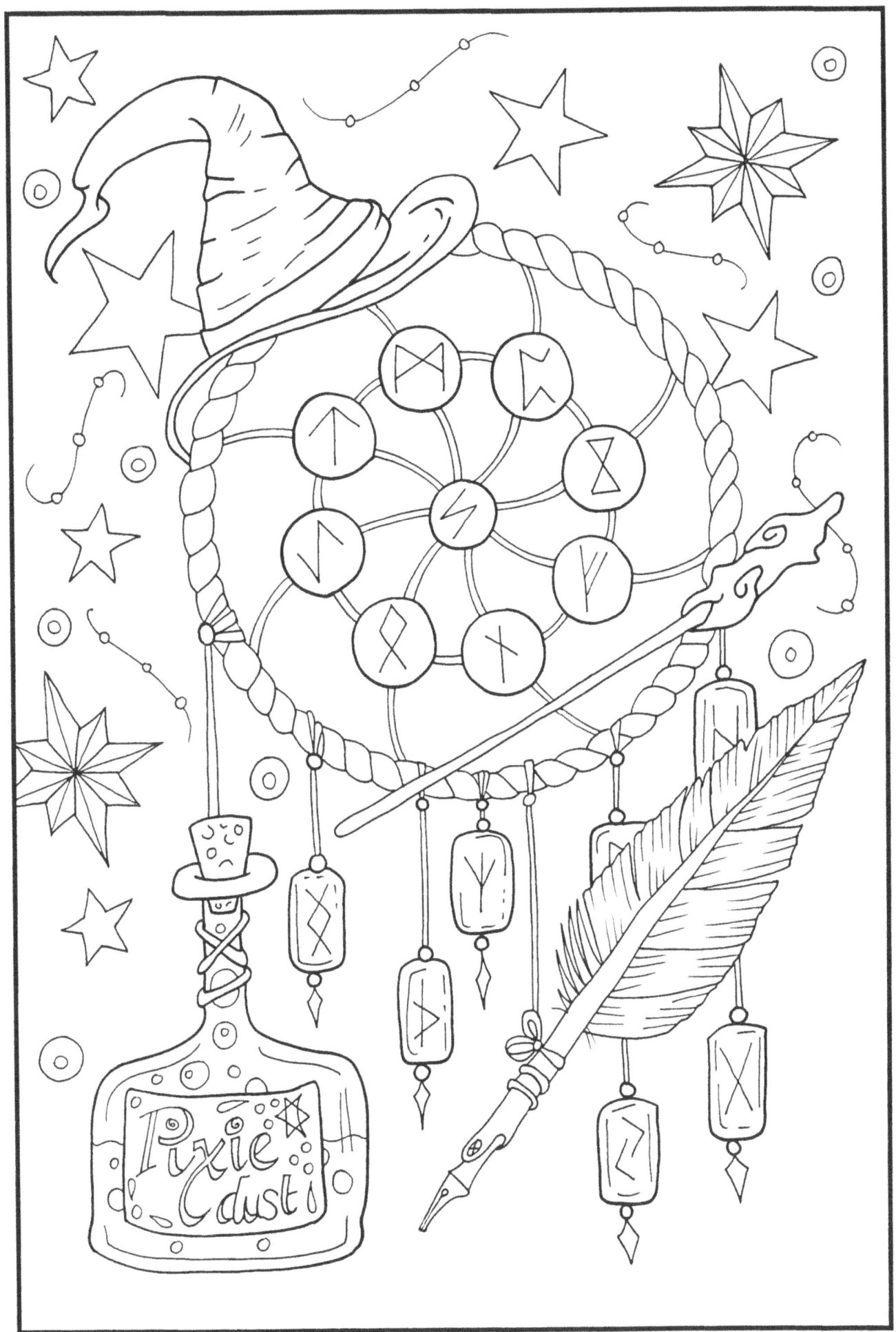

Spellbound

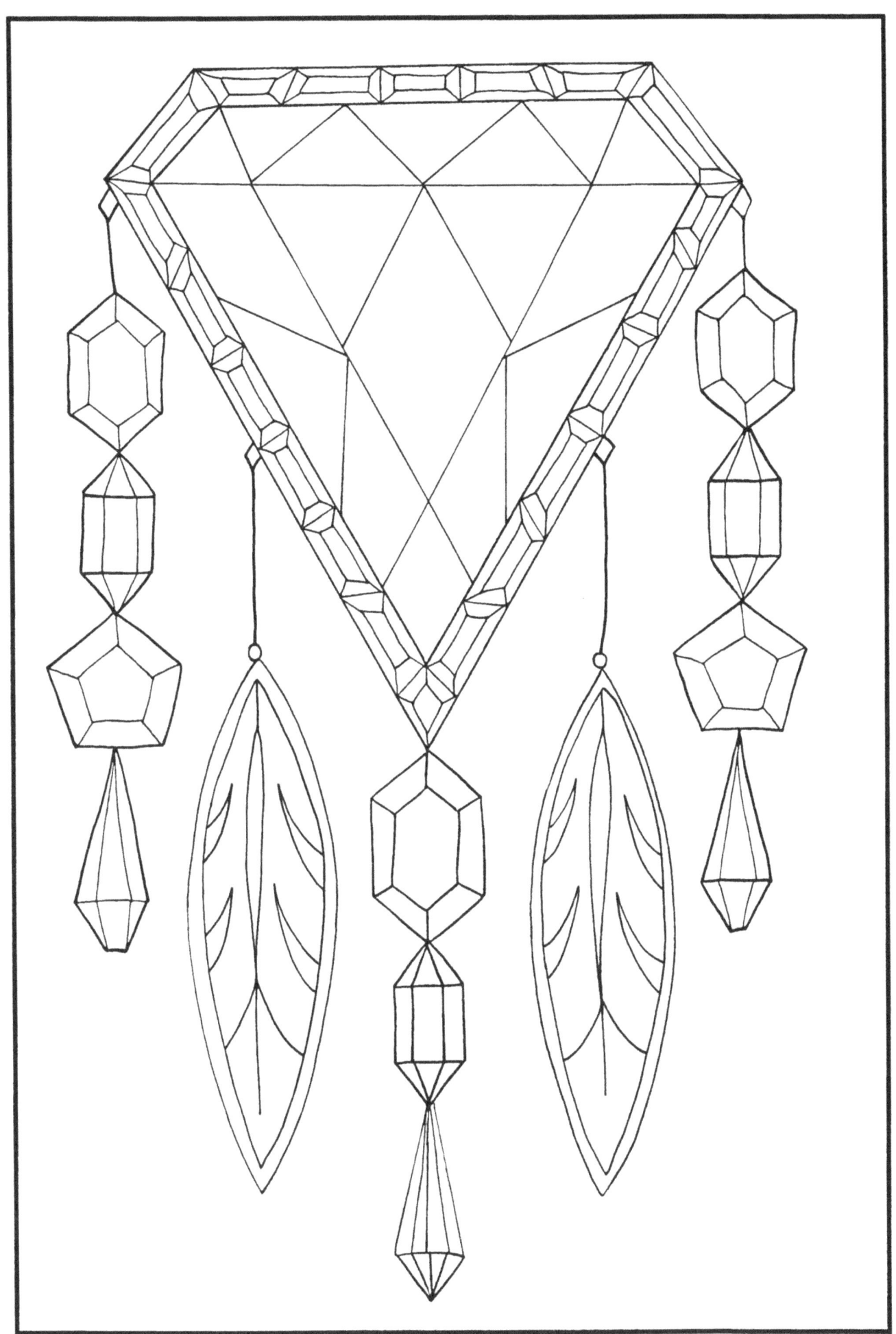

Diamonds and Dreams

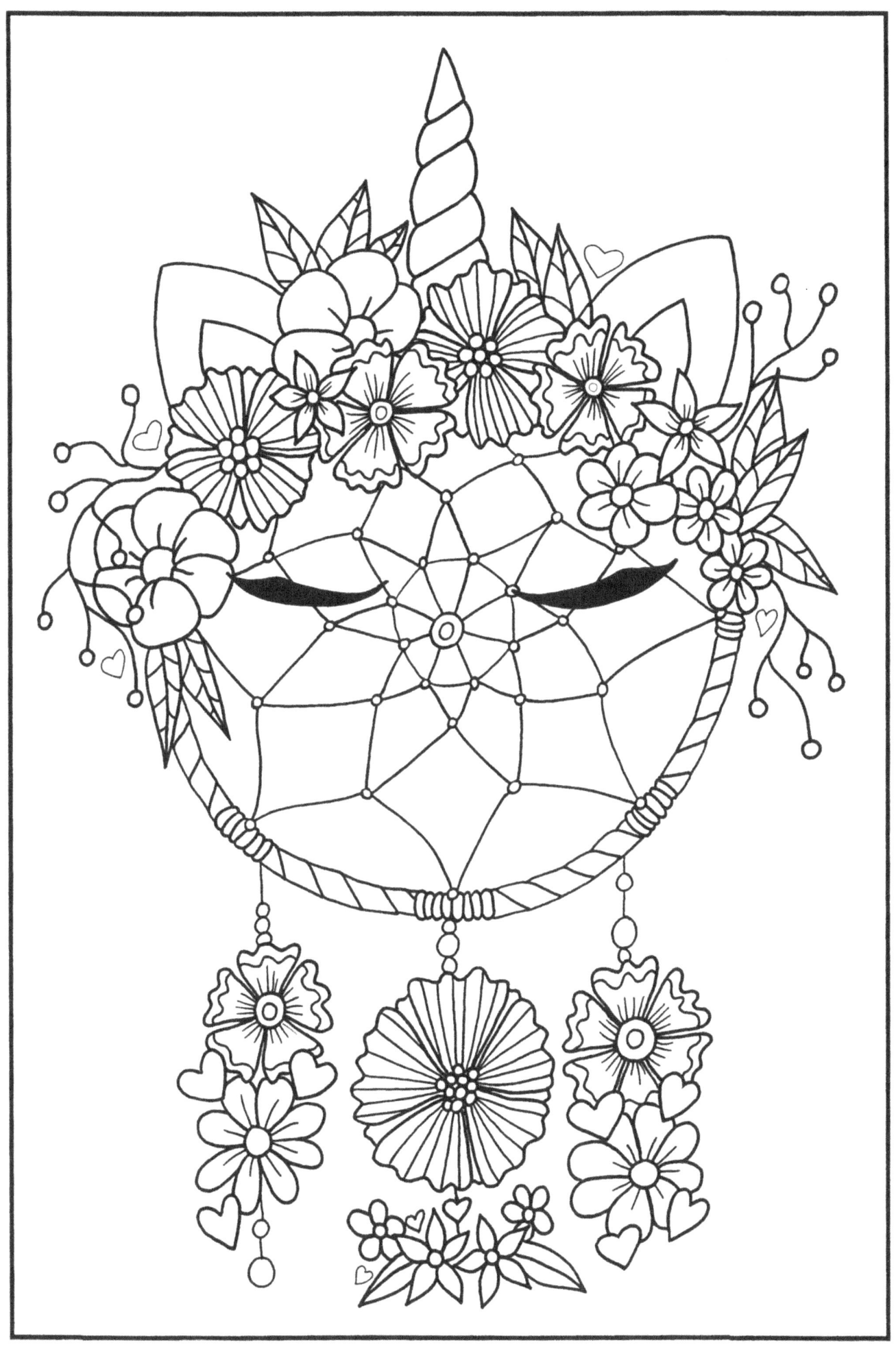

Fantasy Dreams

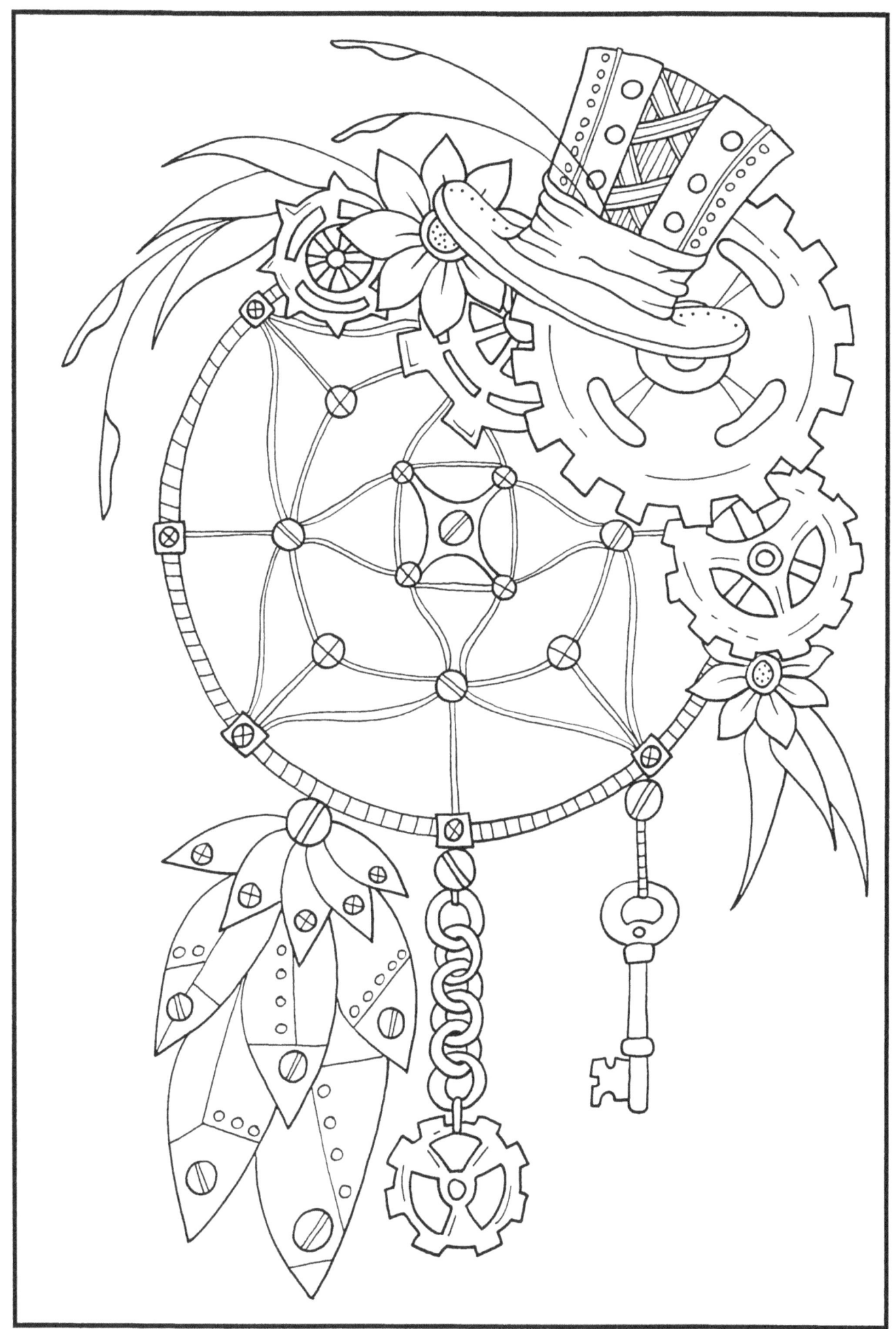

Steampunk

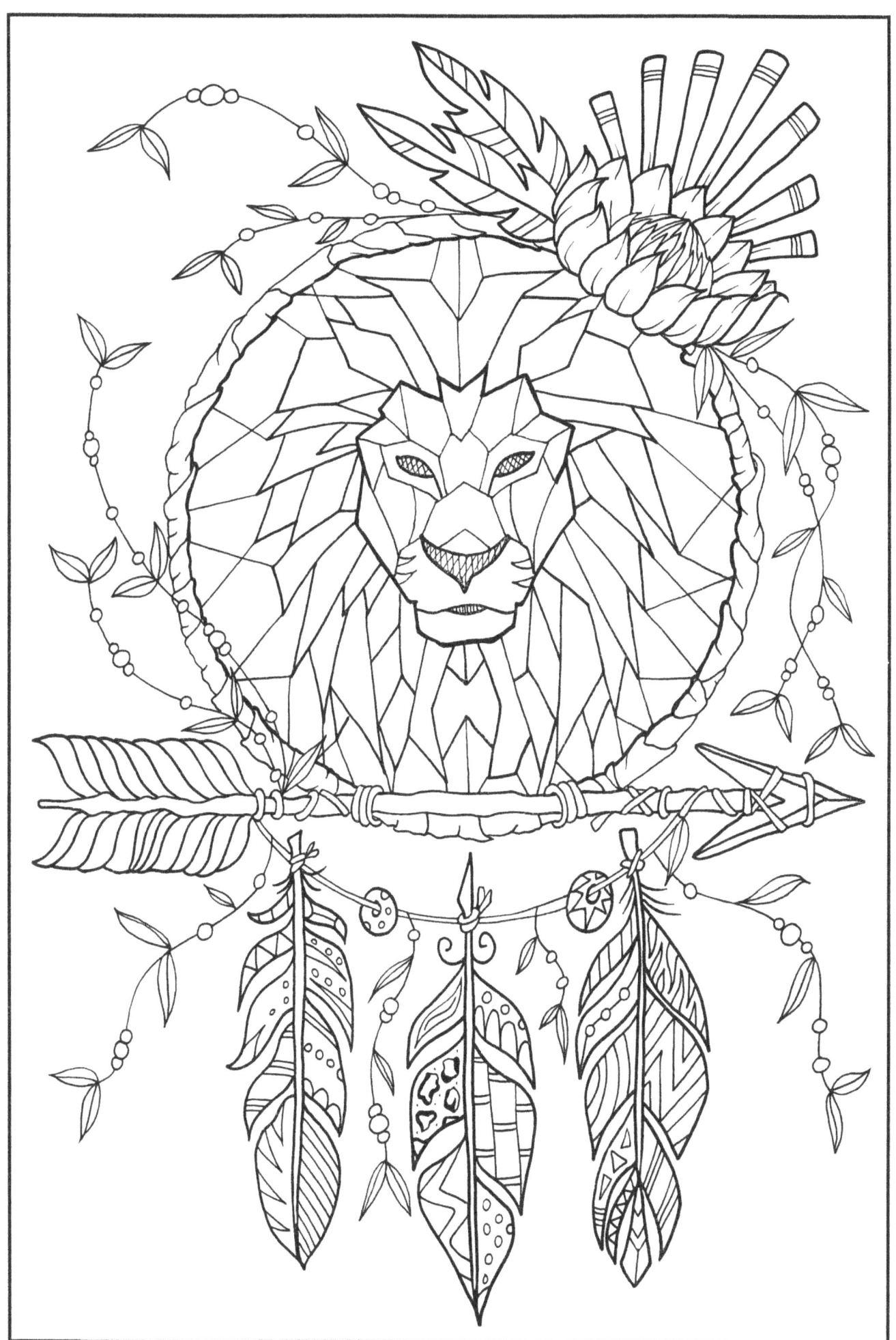

King of the Dreams

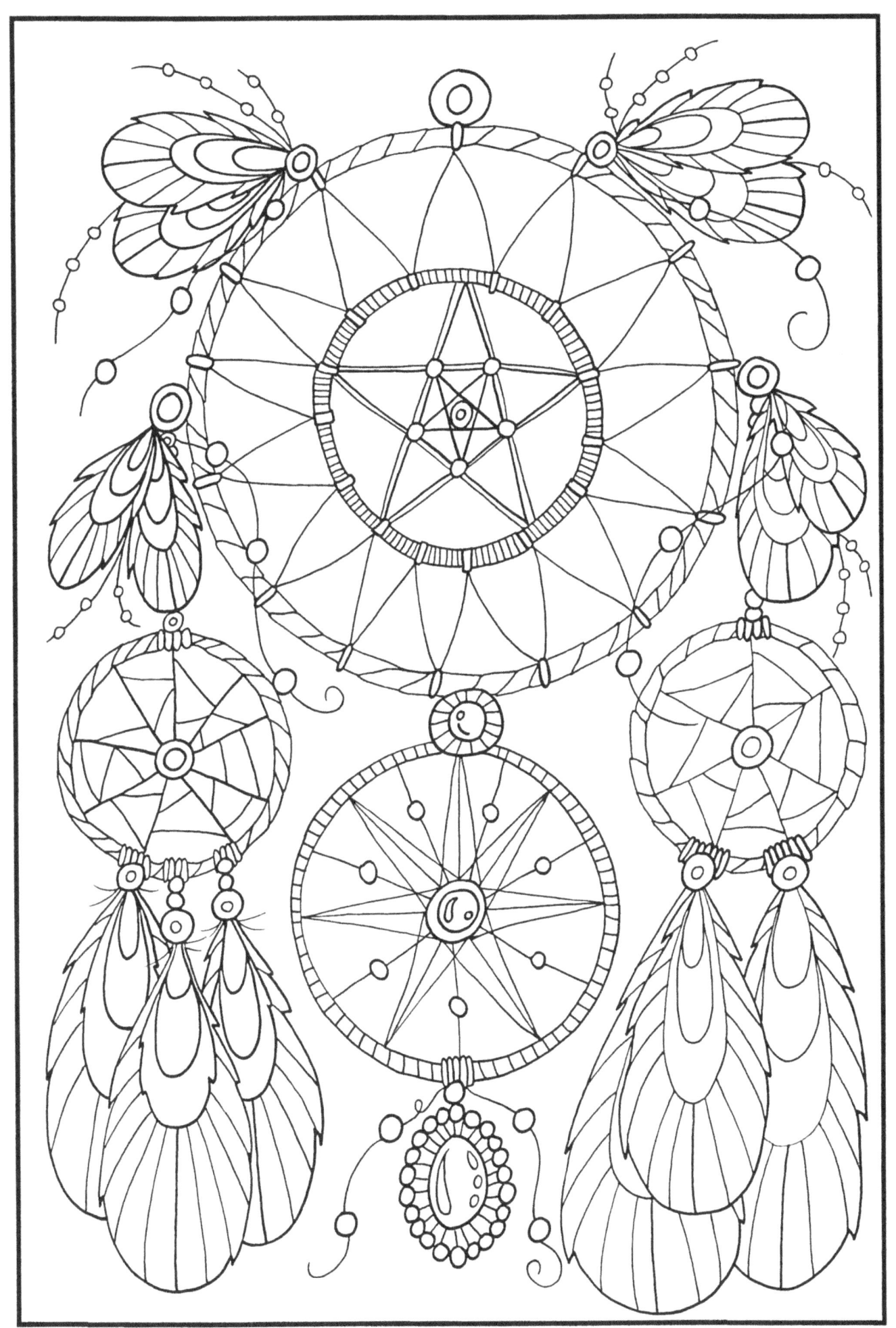

Traditional Dreams

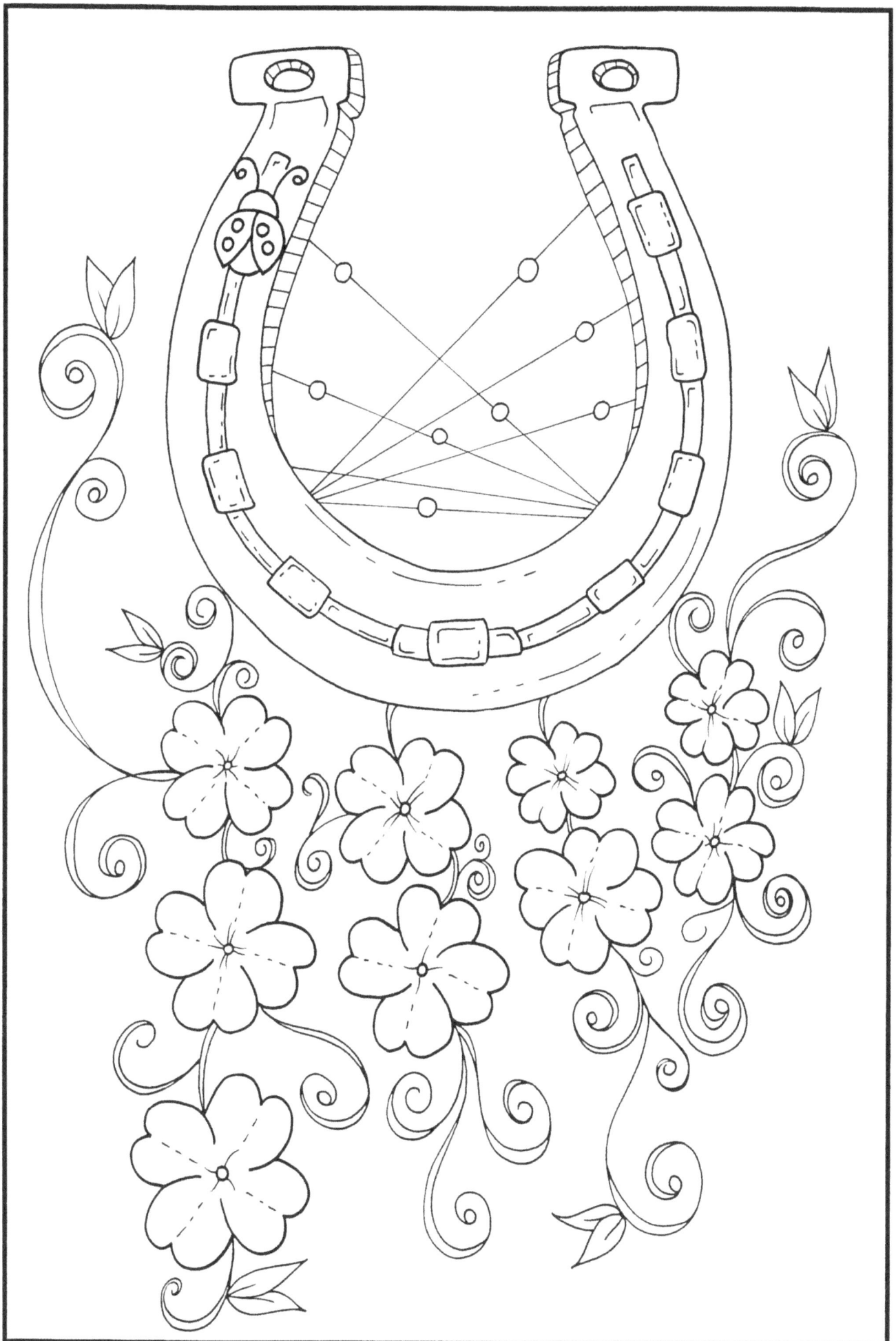

Lucky Dreams

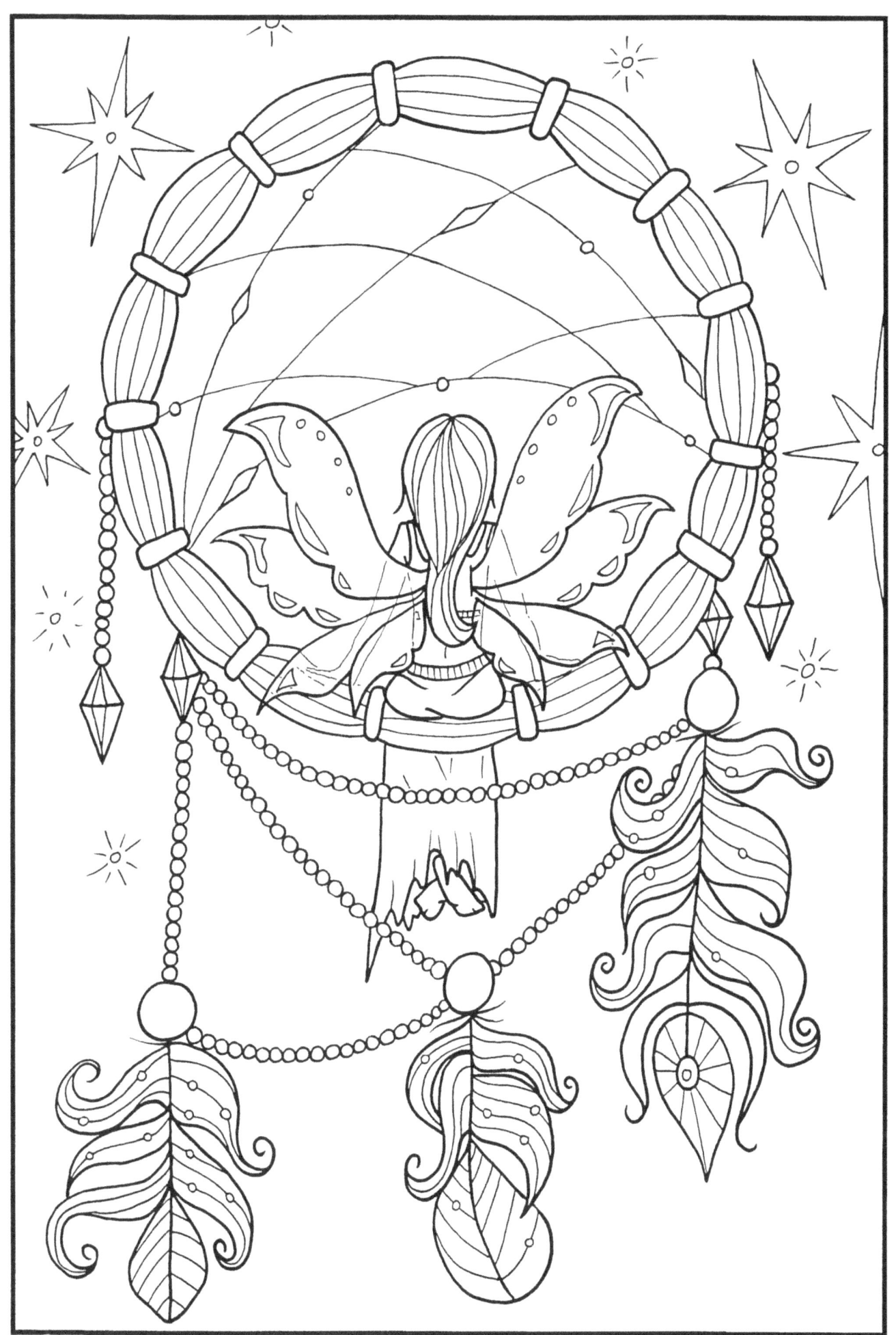

Contemplating Dreams

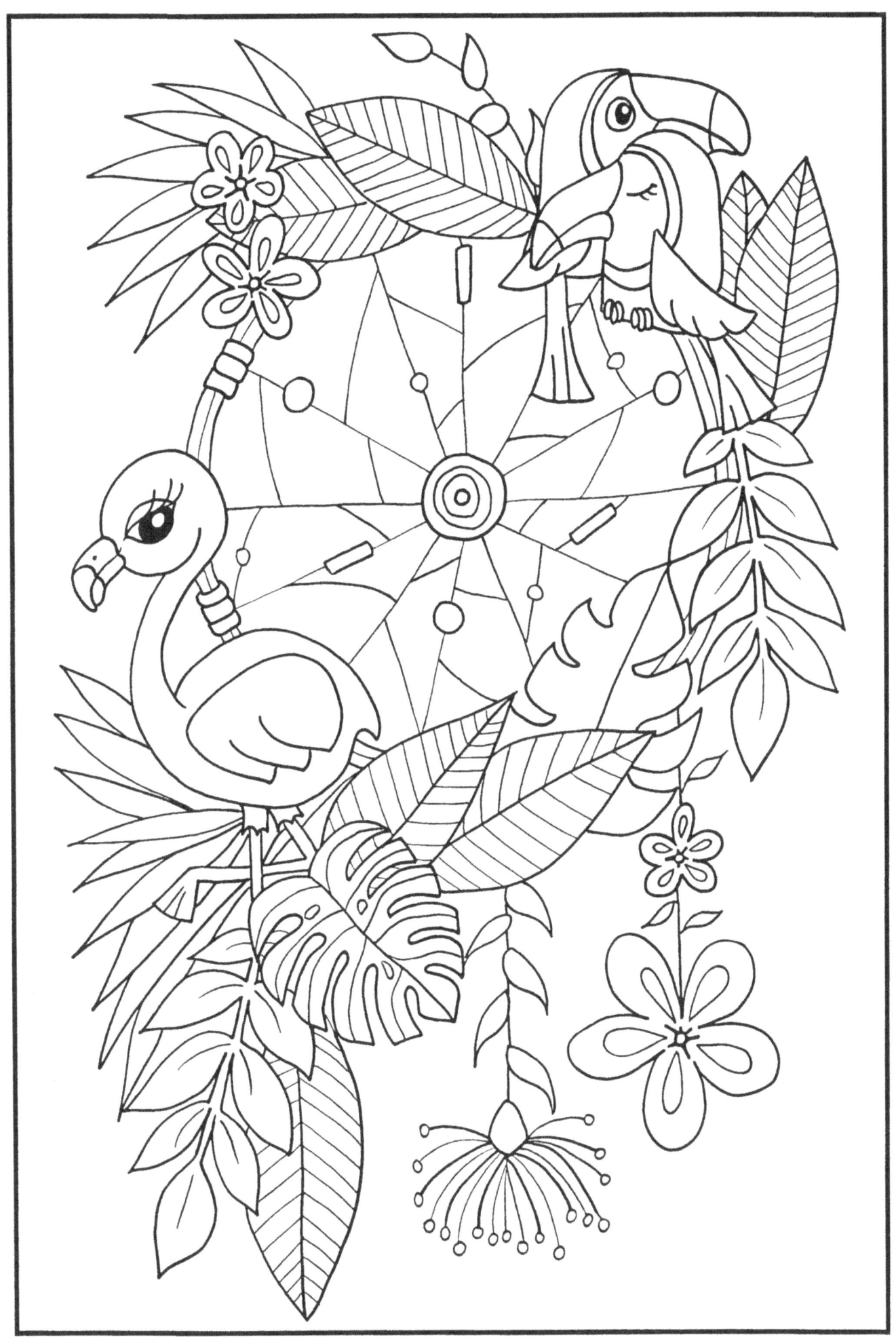

Birds of a Feather

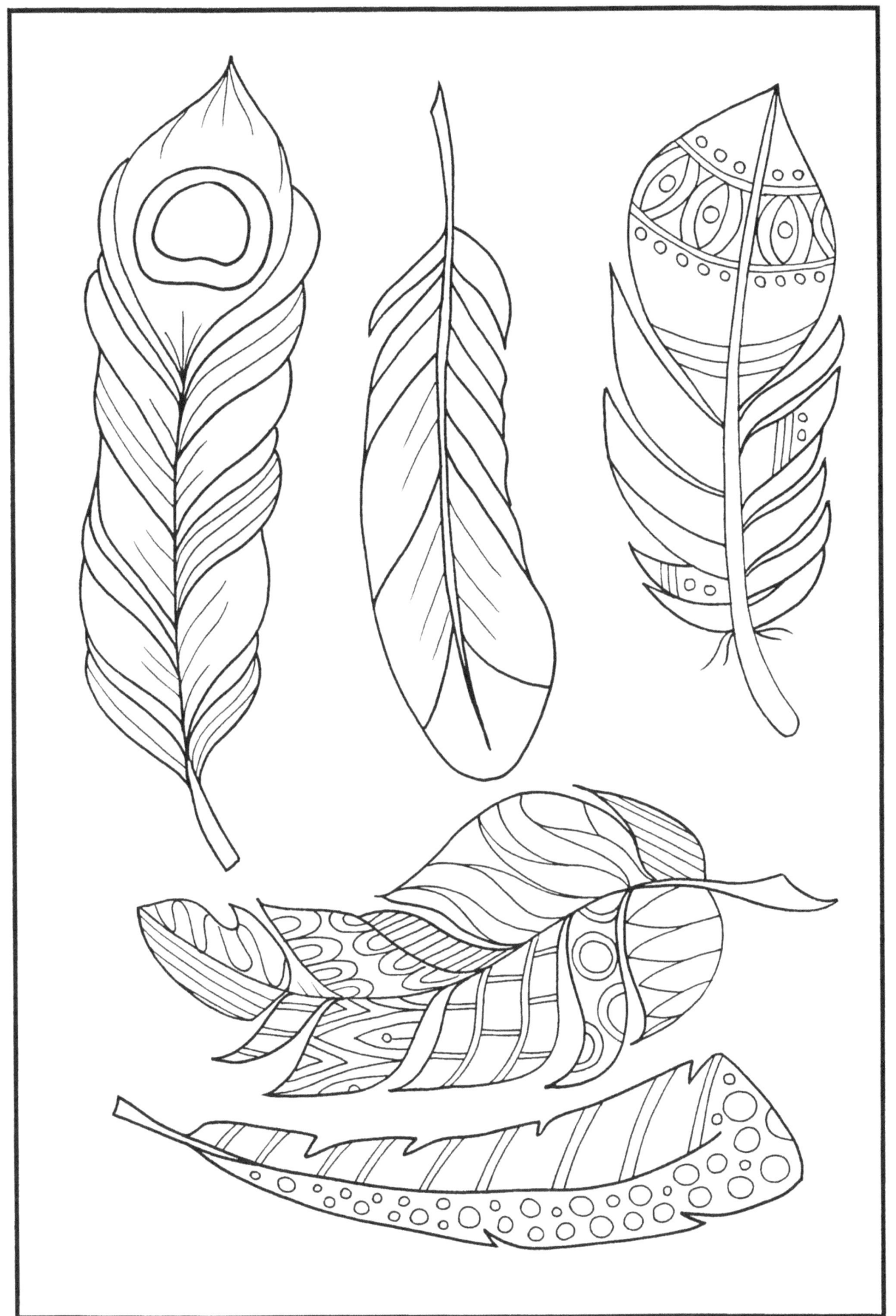

Feathers

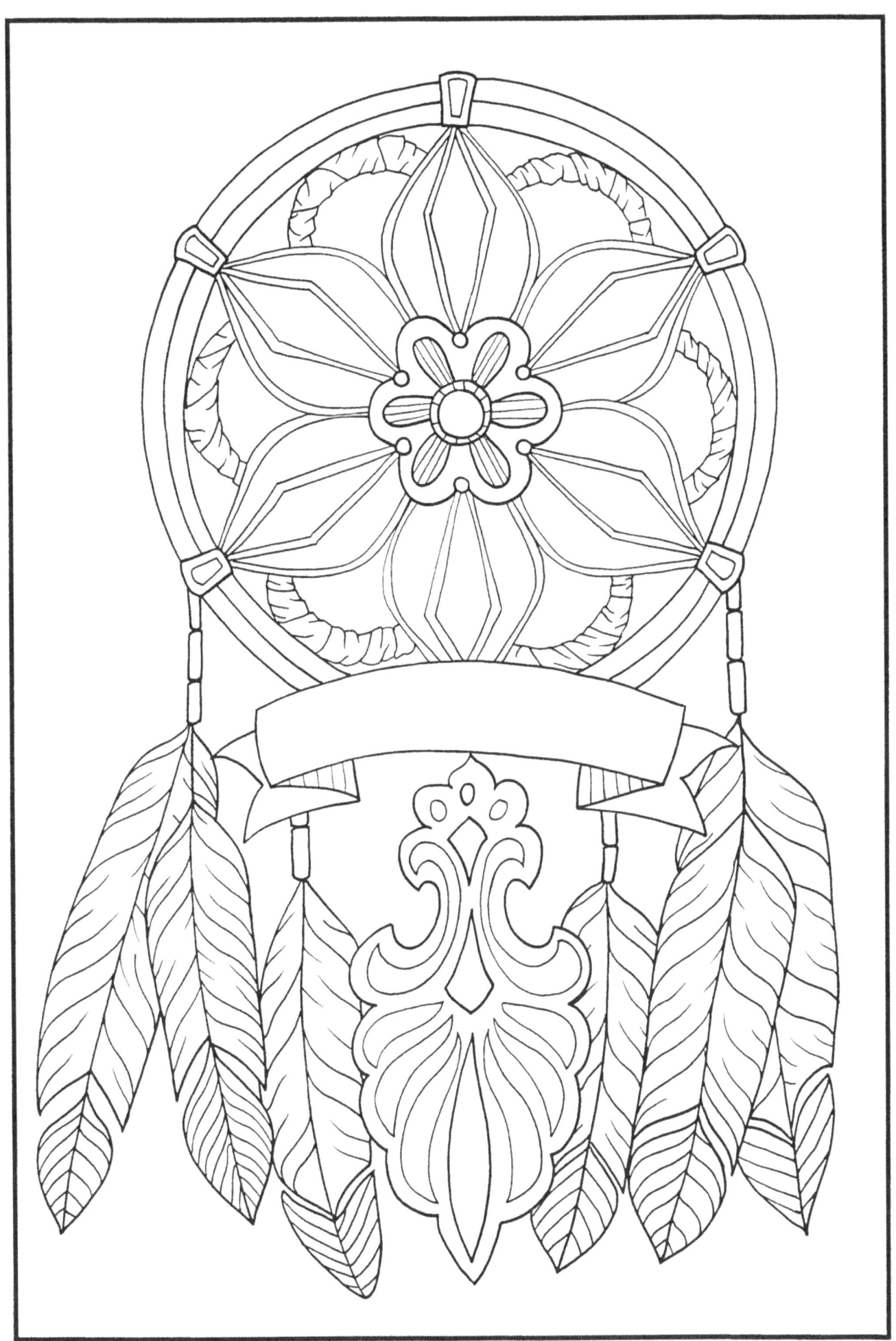

Name your Dreams

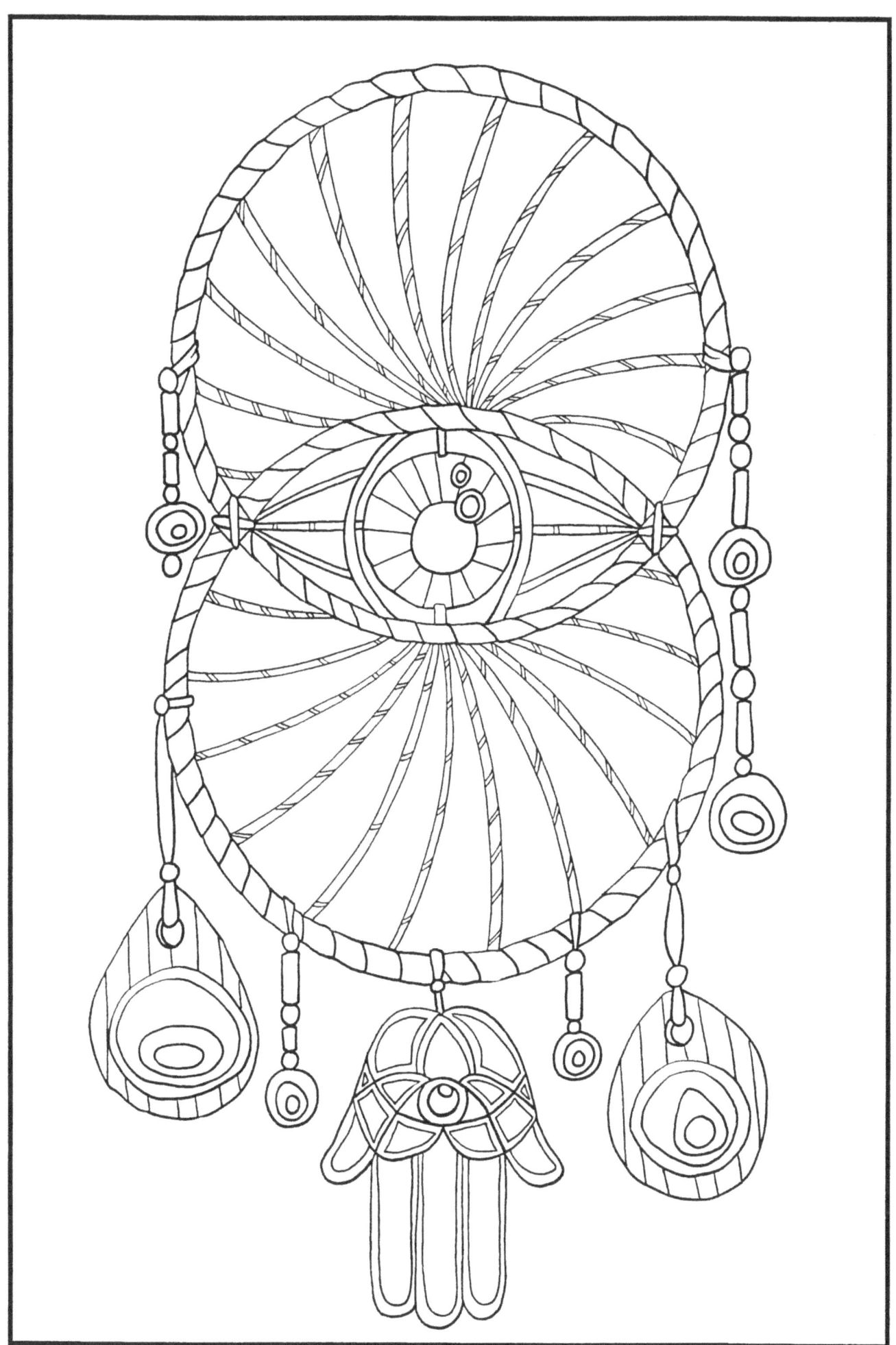

Protective Dreams

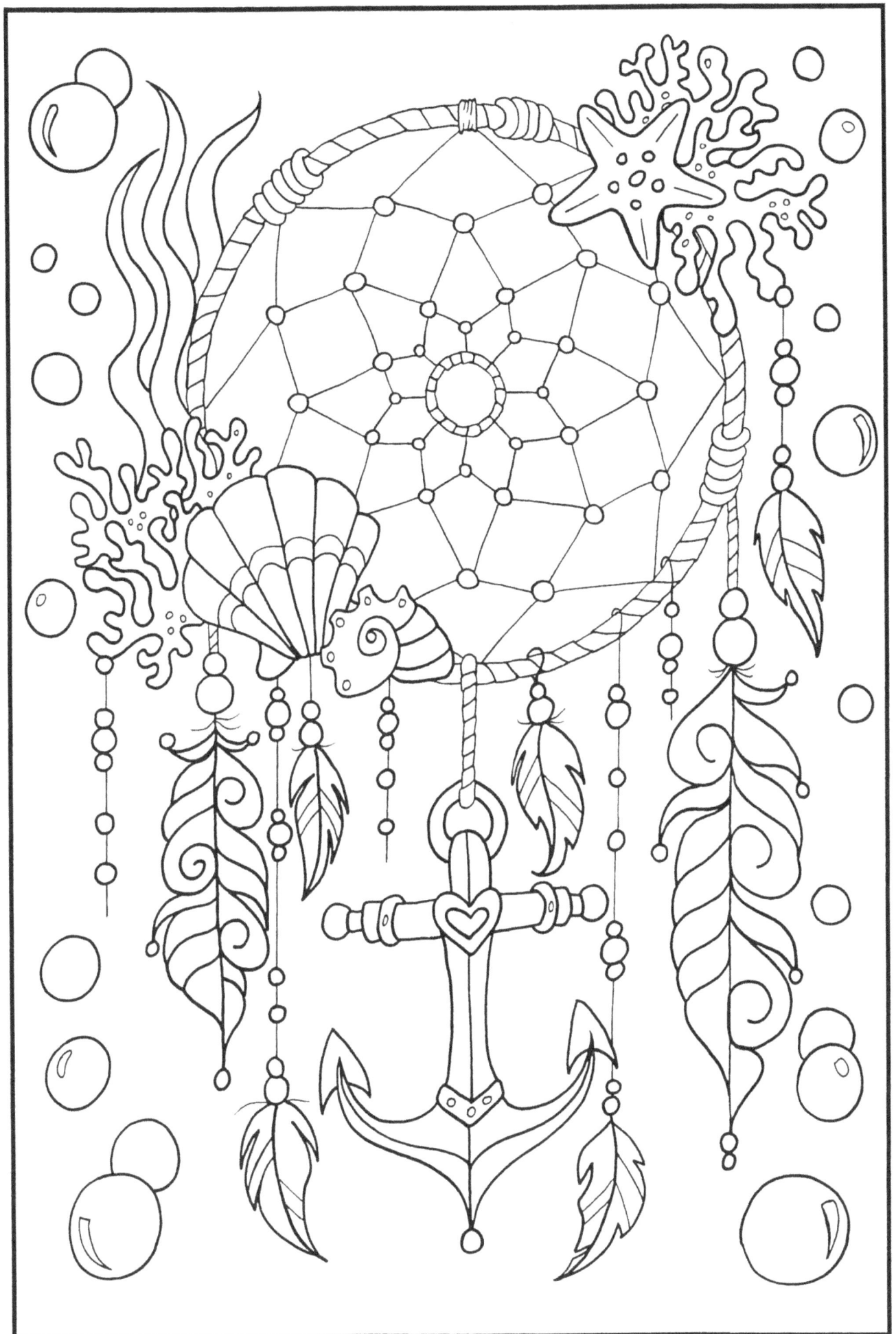

Underwater Dreams

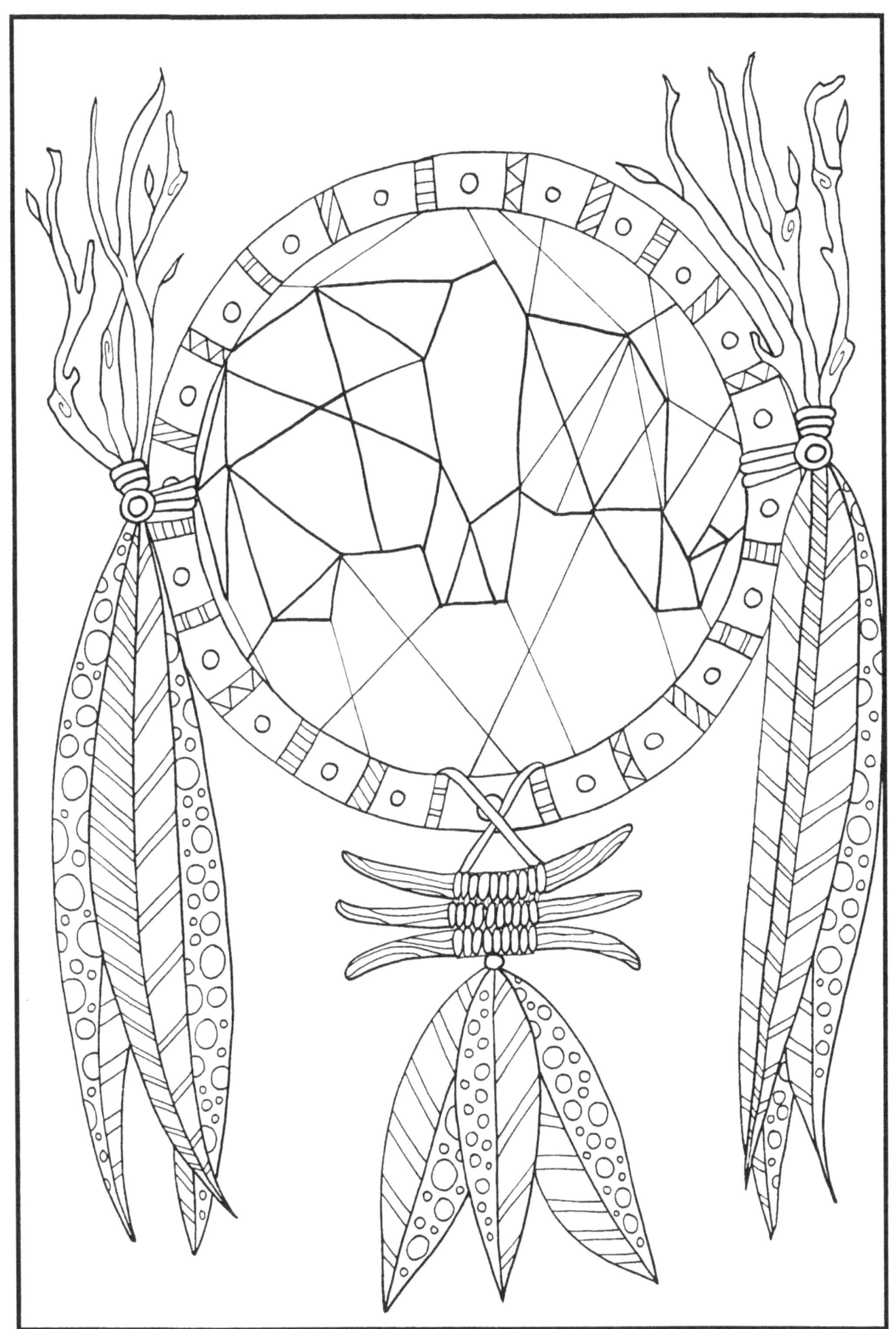

African Dreams

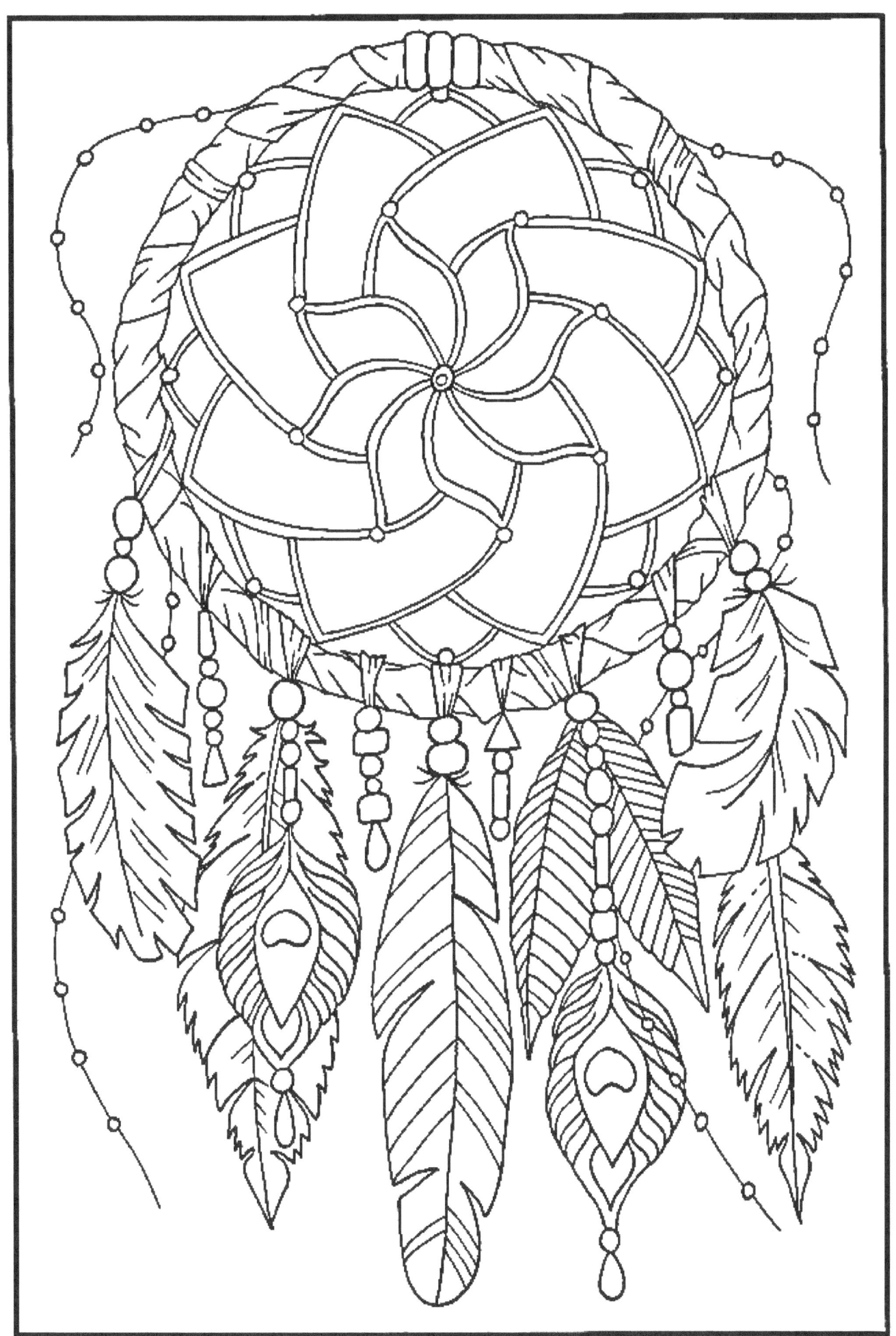

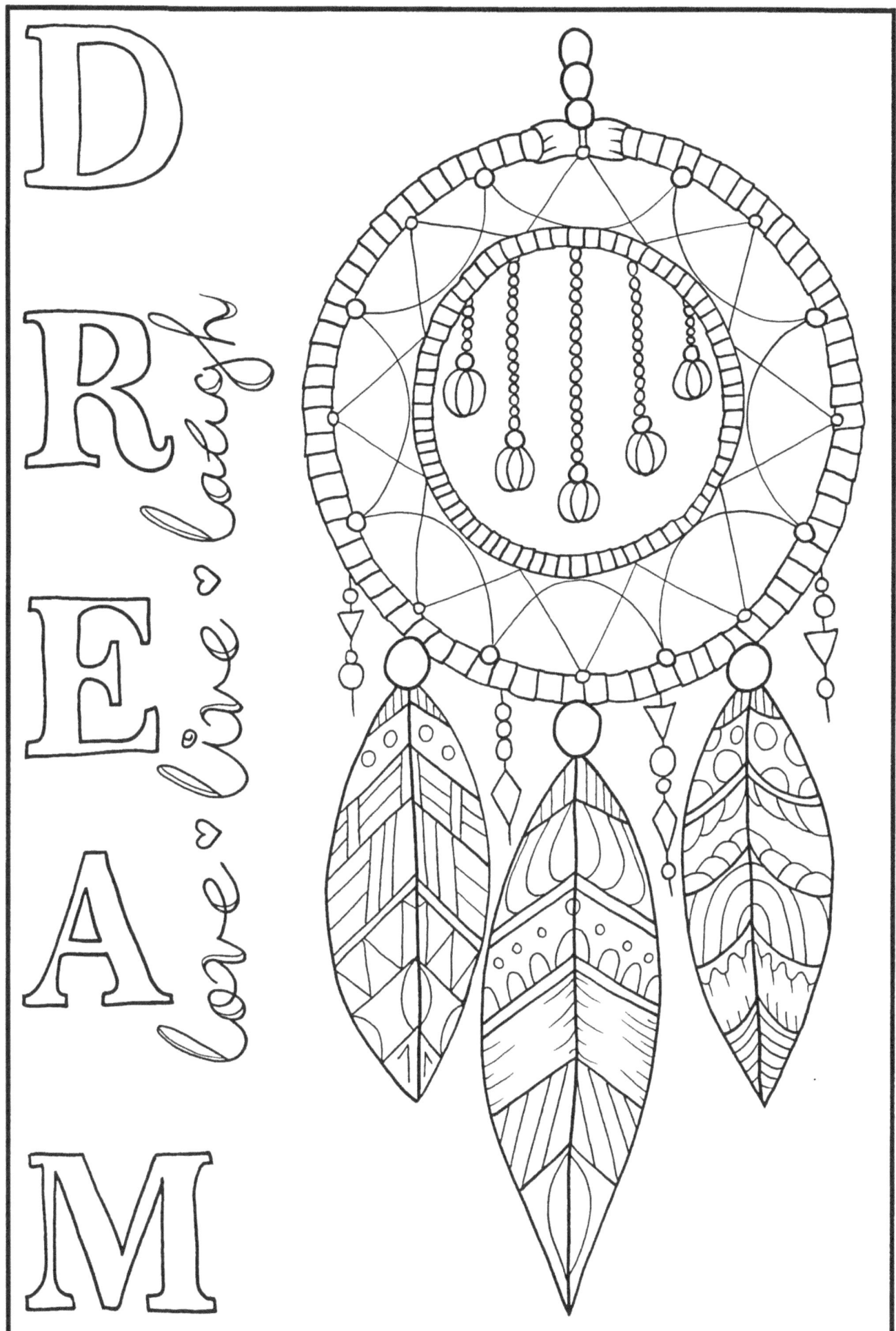

Love – Live – Laugh

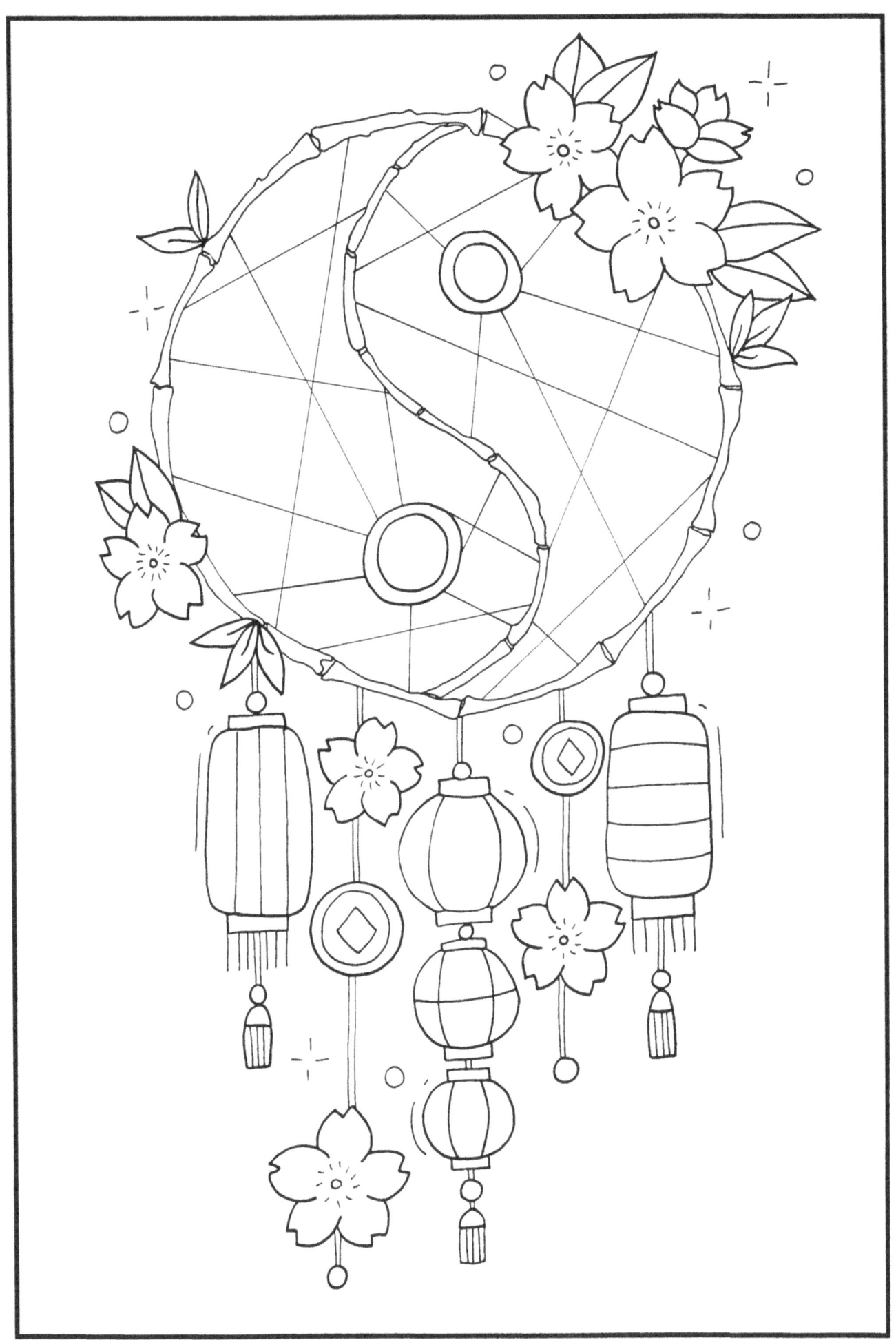

Oriental Dreams

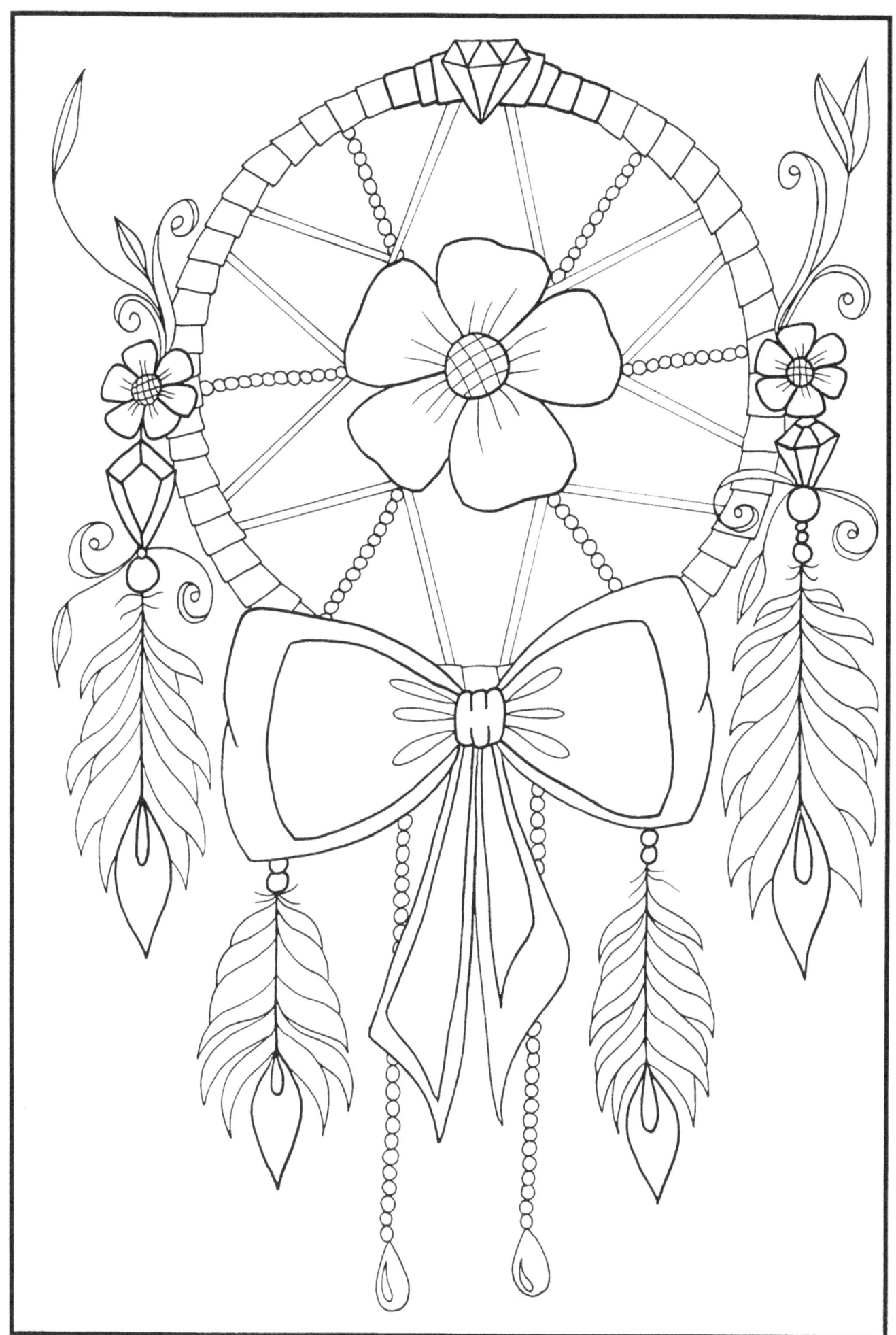

Feathers, Bows and Flowers

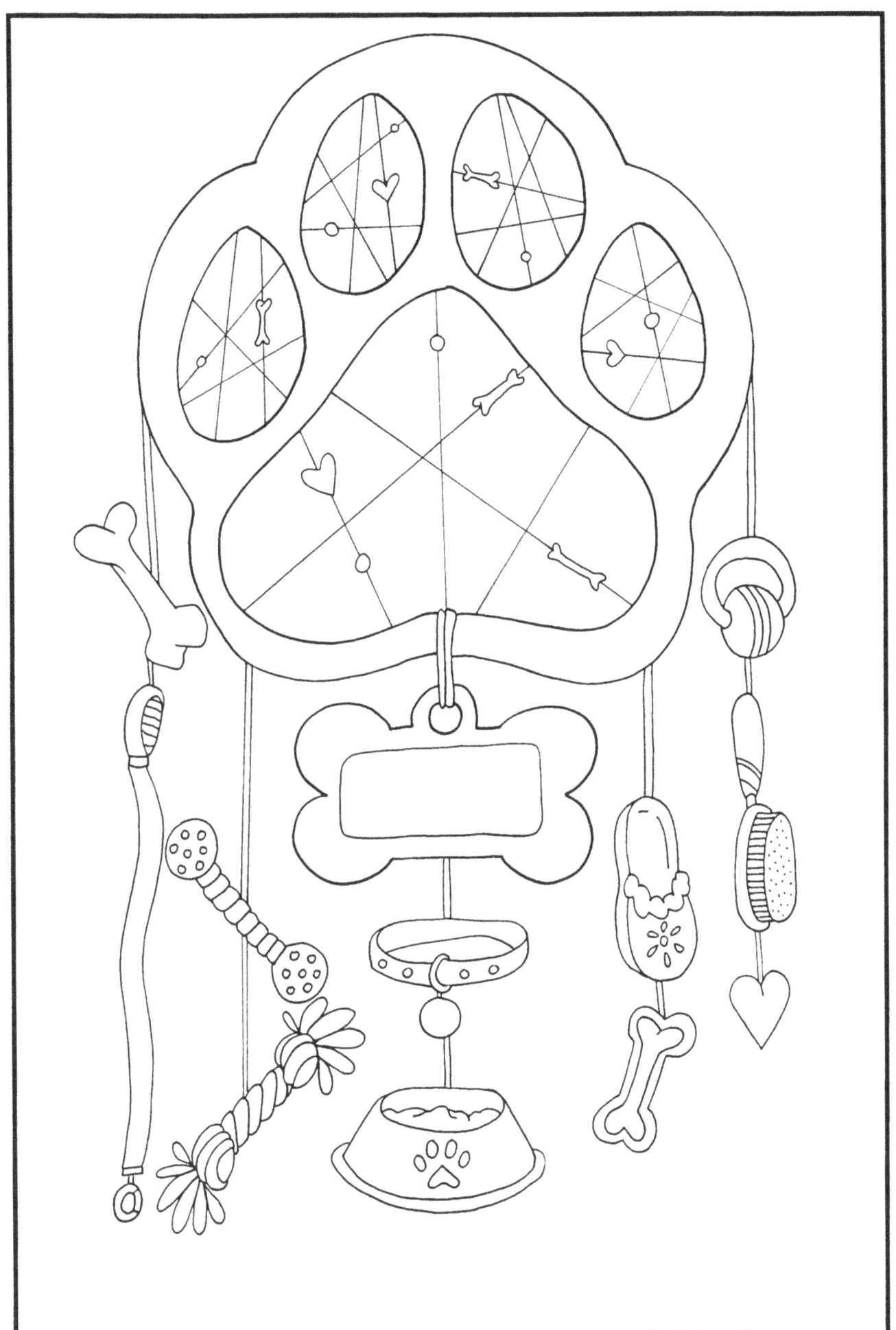

Dogs

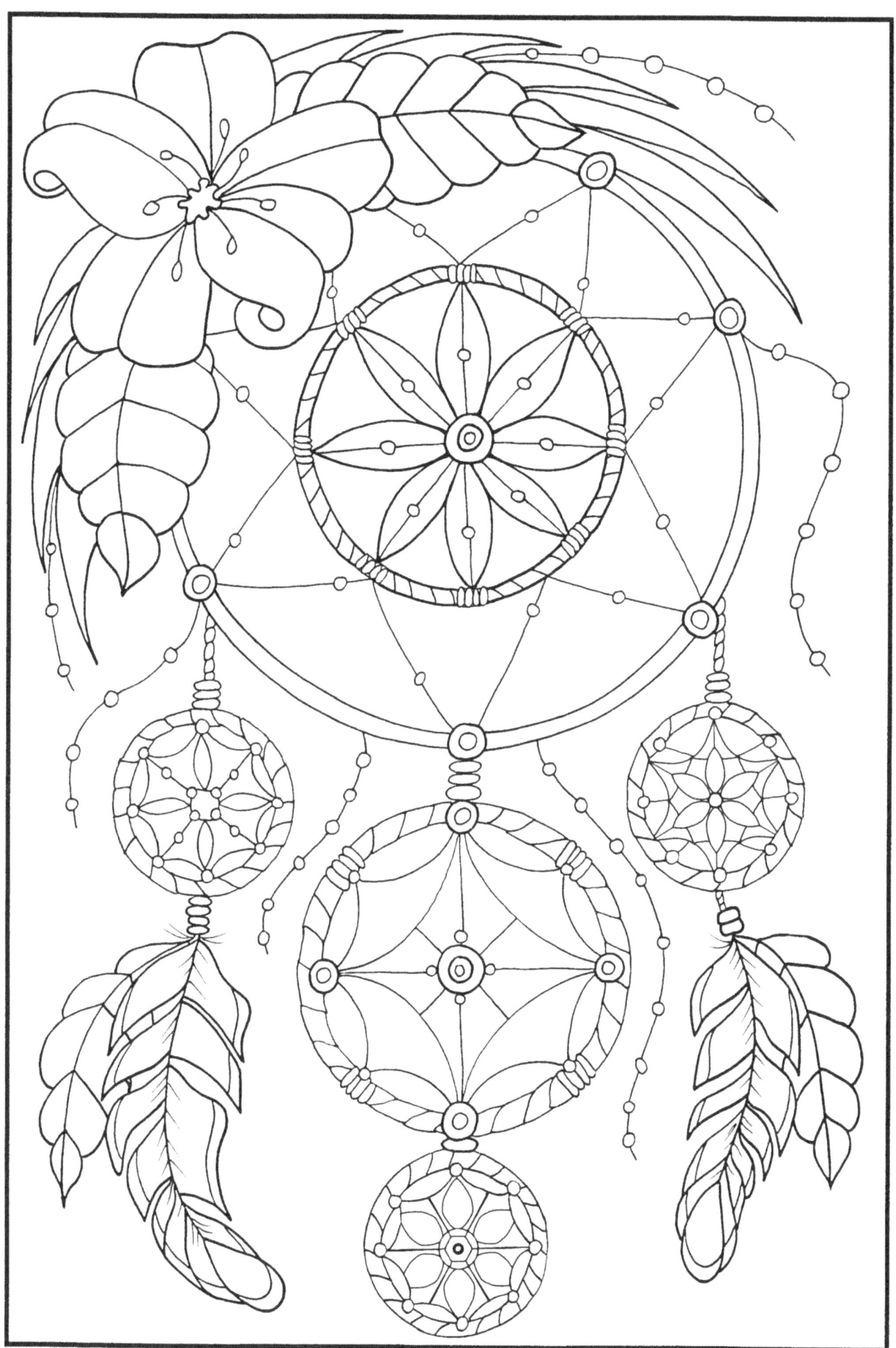

Dream the Dream

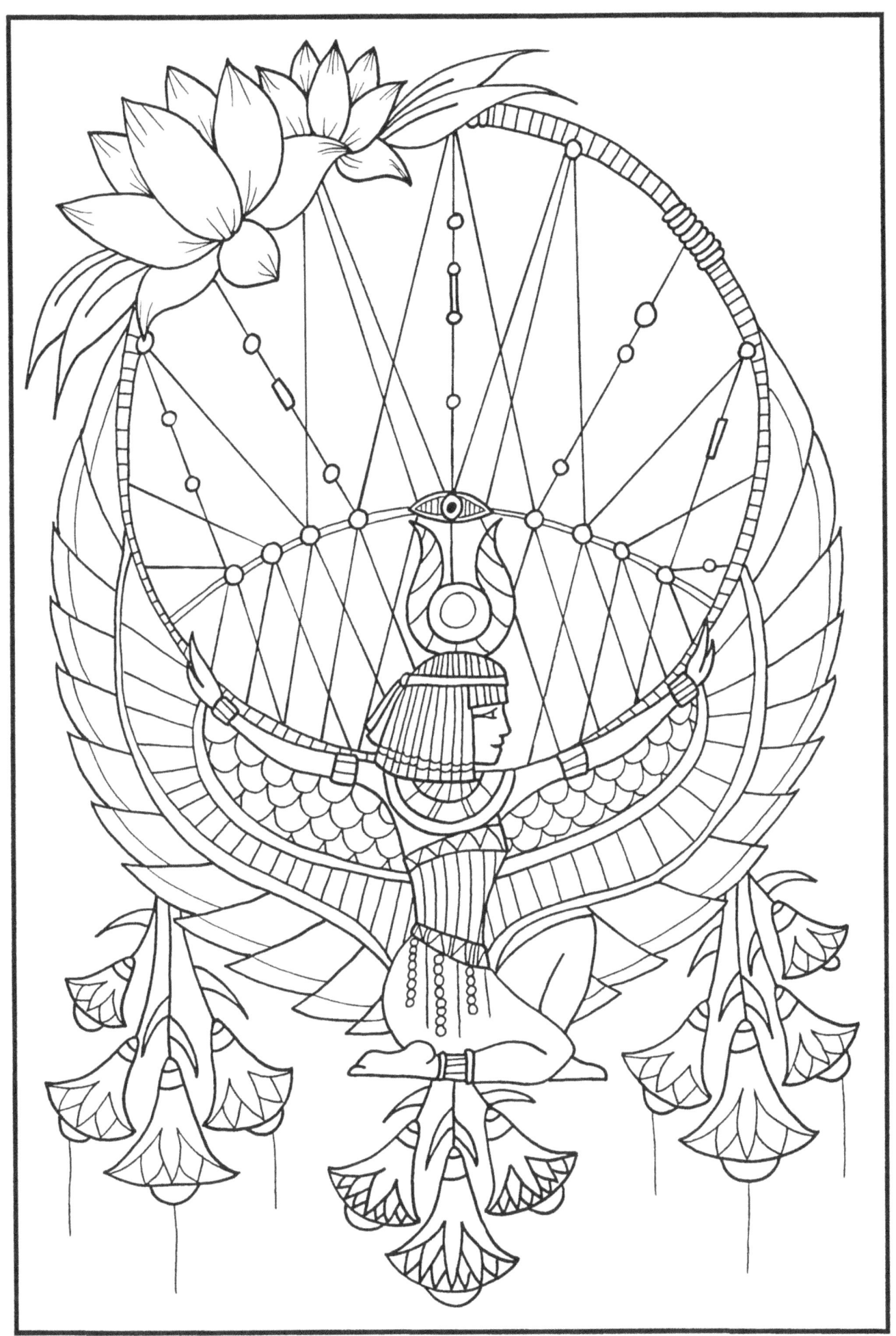

Egyptian Dreams

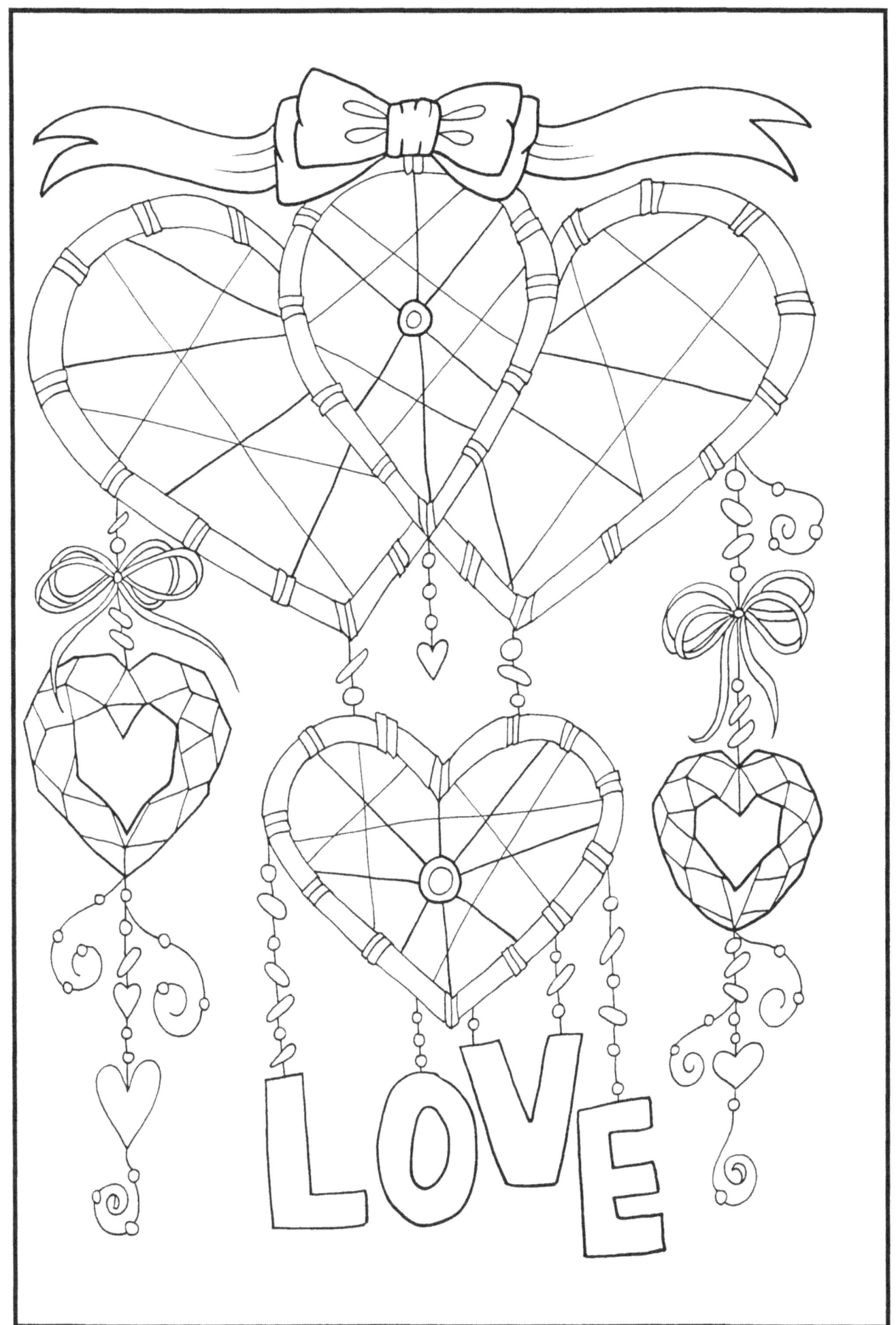

The Dream of Love

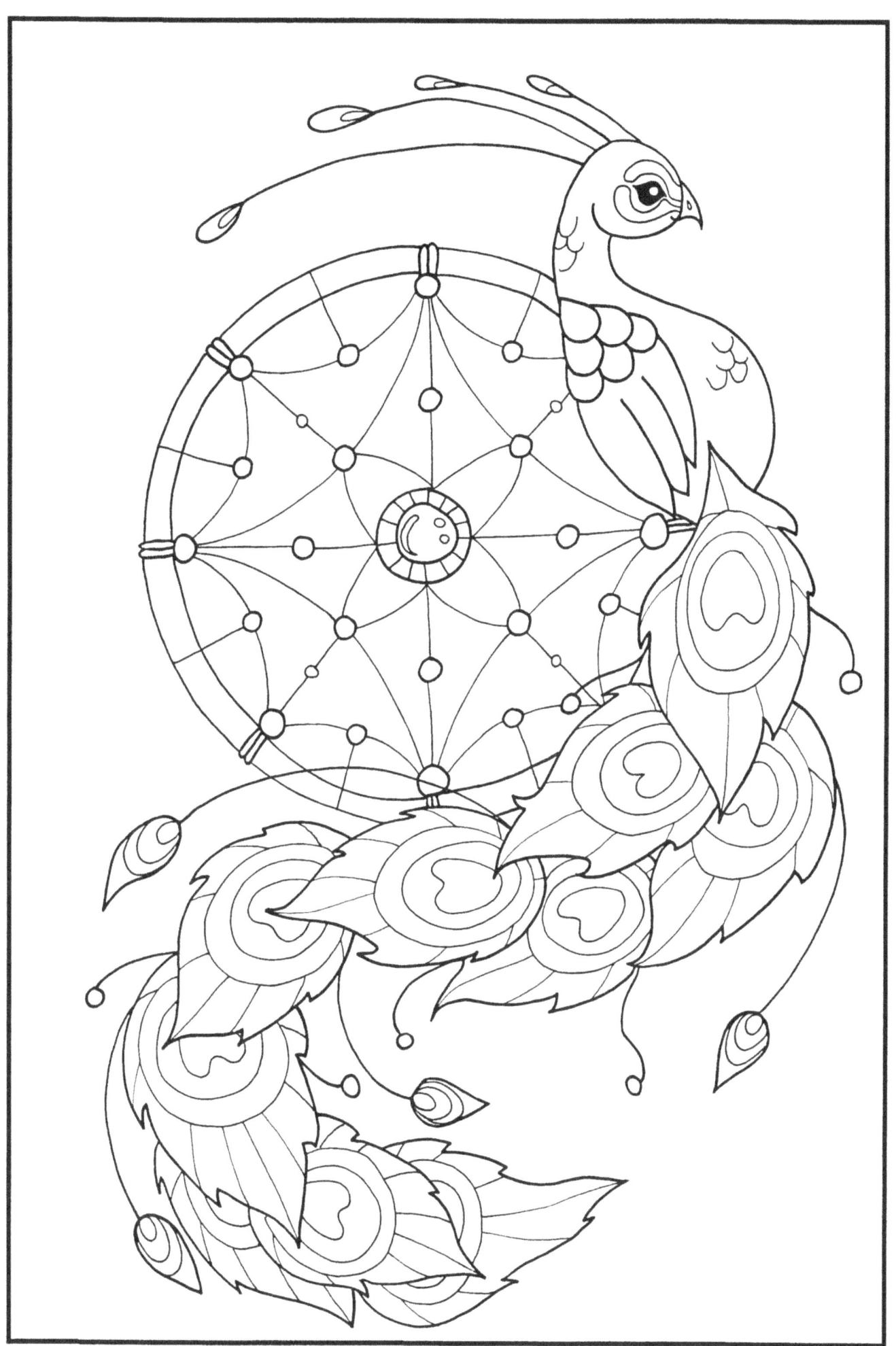

Pretty Dreams

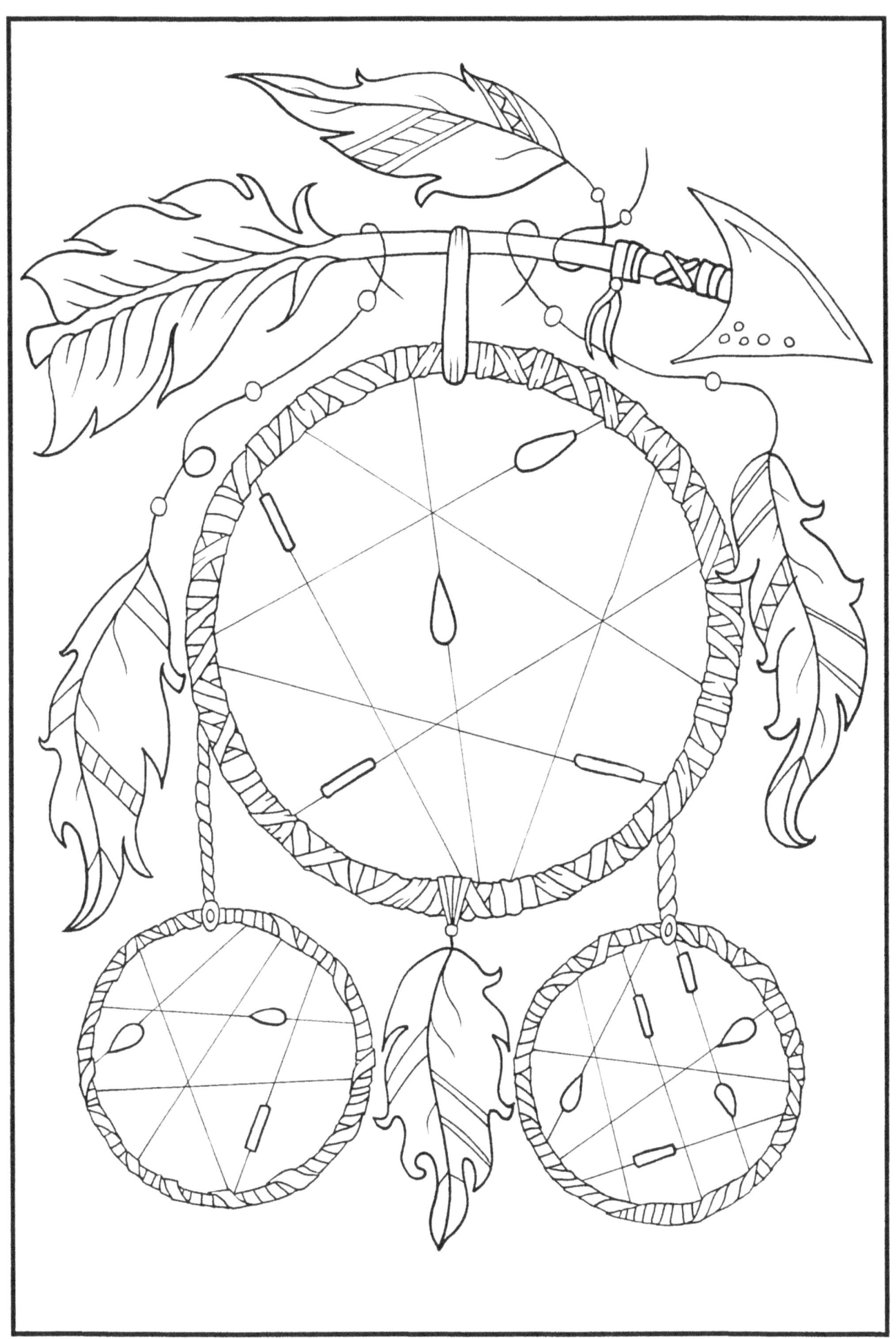

Dreams

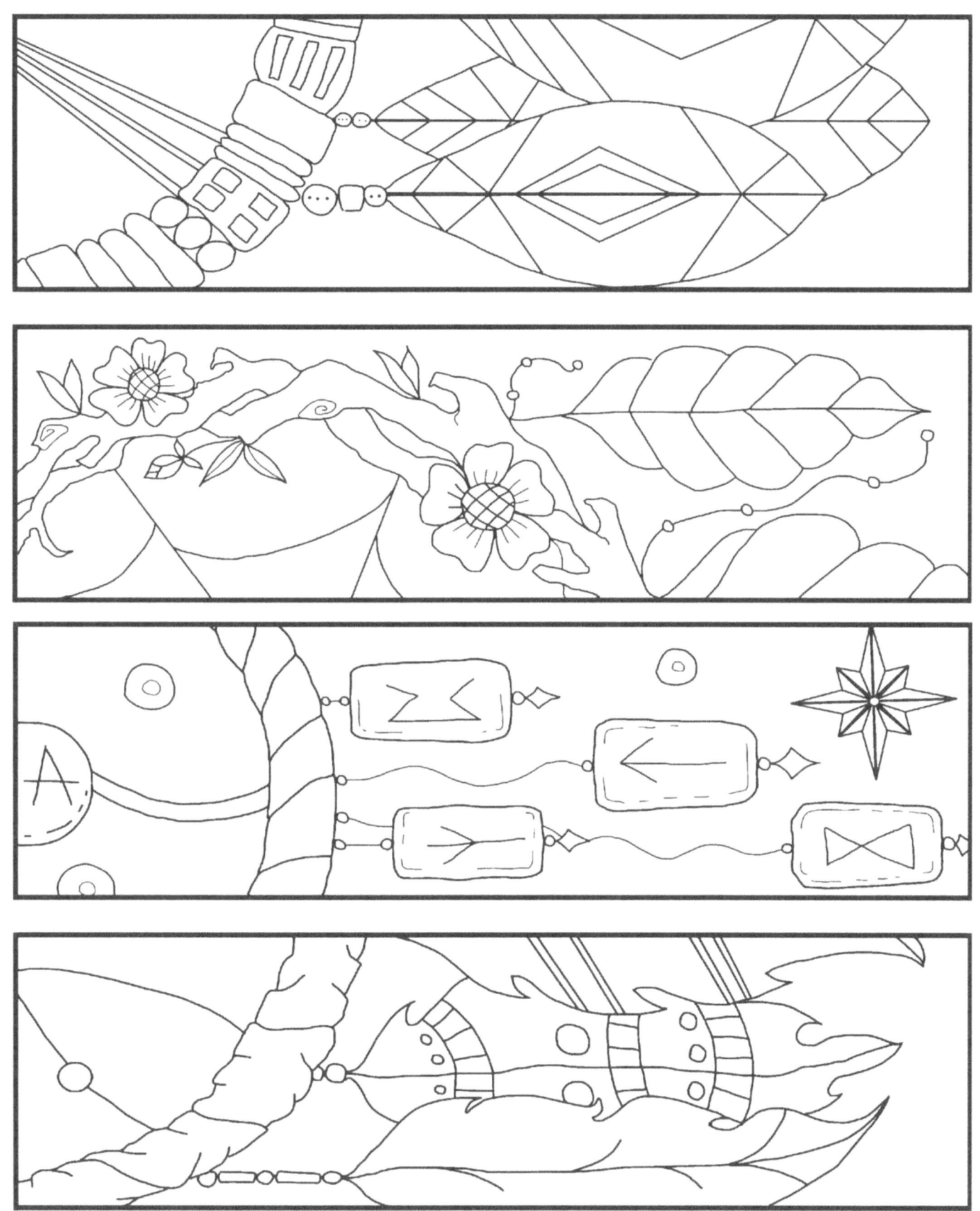

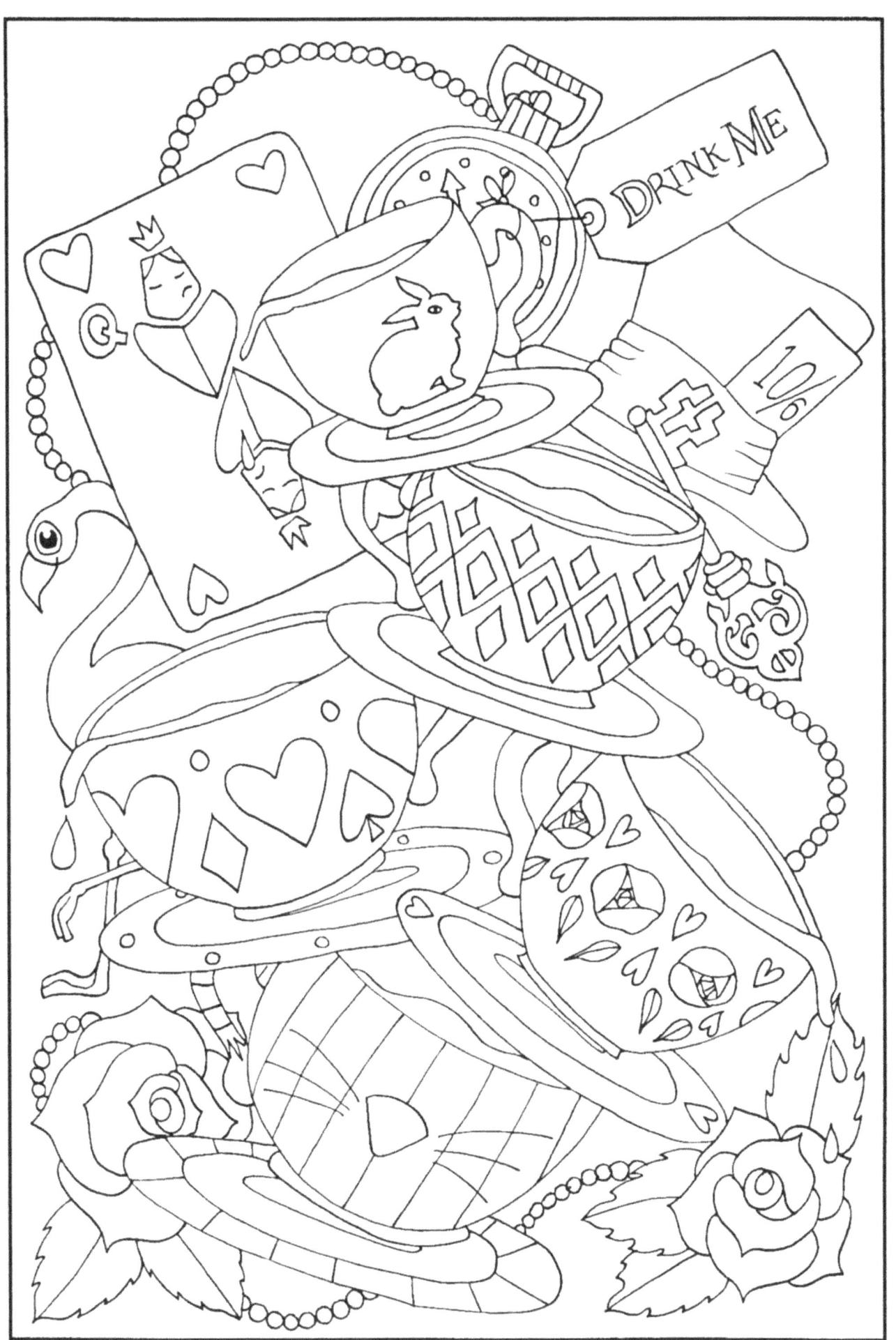

Alice in Wonderland
From book 'FANTASY & FAIRYTALE'

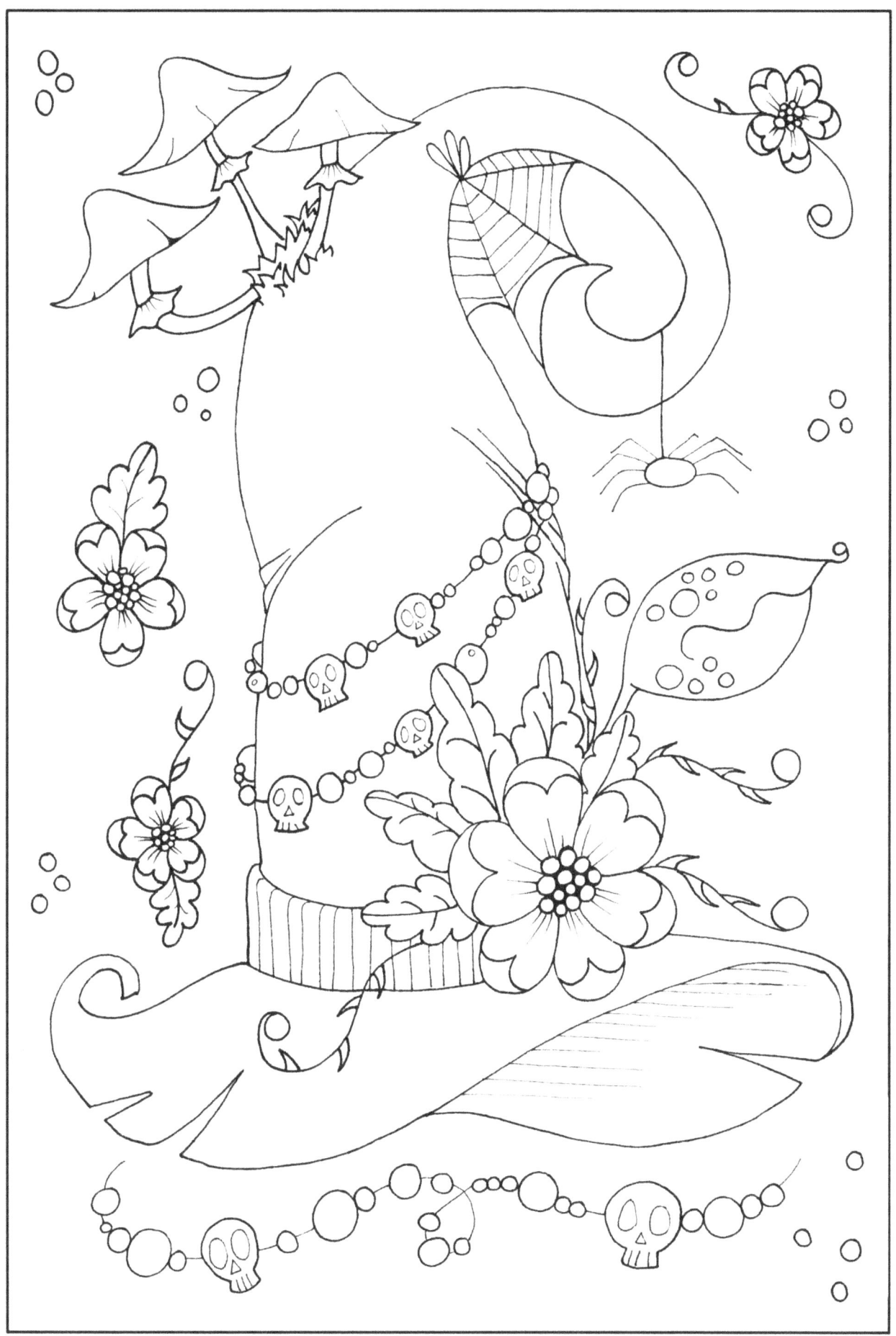

Hats off
From book 'HAPPY HALLOWEEN'

www.ingramcontent.com/pod-product-compliance
Lightning Source LLC
Chambersburg PA
CBHW081741220526
45468CB00008B/2190